ROGERS' RULES
for
BUSINESSWOMEN

ROGERS' RULES
for
BUSINESSWOMEN:

HOW TO START
A CAREER
AND MOVE UP
THE LADDER

Henry C. Rogers

ST. MARTIN'S PRESS
NEW YORK

Design by Katherine Urban

Library of Congress Cataloging-in-Publication Data

Rogers, Henry C.
  [Rules for business women]
  Rogers' rules for business women / Henry C. Rogers.
    p.   cm.
  ISBN 0-312-01081-8
  1. Success in business. 2. Women in business. 3. Career
development. 4. Psychology, Industrial. I. Title.
HF5386.R54448 1988
650.1'024042—dc19   88-16889
                                                        CIP

First Edition
10 9 8 7 6 5 4 3 2 1

To Melissa:
  Who cautioned, "Don't talk down to us,
  Grandpa."
  I have followed her advice.

Contents

Foreword

As we look into the future to the 1990s there will no longer be books advising women in business on how to become successful. The scores of books on this subject currently in every major book store will gradually disappear from the shelves to be replaced by a new literature— "How *You* Can Become Successful." These will be books written for *people*, not for women or for men. This change will take place because we are now in a state of transition between the thousand-year-long predominance of the male in the workplace to that glorious day when women can look at the American business community and proudly say, "All men and women are created equal and they are equal."

This present state of transition came about as a result of the women's liberation movement led by Betty Friedan, Germaine Greer, Gloria Steinem, Bella Abzug, et al, and exploded in the early sixties. The movement grew until today the "old boy network" is forced to compete numerically with the "old girl network." Sex discrimination was an accepted tradition only a quarter of a century ago, and is still with us in some industries and geographical areas. But there are more women working today in management positions than ever before, and the gap between the male and the female wage scale is shrinking year by year. Sexual harassment is another barrier to sexual equality that is rapidly eroding, not only because women will no longer accept it, but because enlightened management in many of our major corporations, such as Xerox, Dupont and Philip Morris, has set up rules of conduct and instituted training sessions on the subject for both men and women. Finally, sex in the workplace, still a taboo subject in many areas of business, has come out of the closet and, gradually, new rules of behavior are gaining a solid foothold.

This time of transition for women in business is studied by Henry Rogers, founder of one of the largest public relations firms in the country. The author of three previous "success" books has now invaded a field previously recognized as the exclusive domain of women writers—a book written for women, advising them how to become successful in the world of business.

Henry Rogers' claim to credibility is based on his experience working with and for some outstanding career women, who were and are his clients, and as an employer of hundreds of women.

Rogers knows what he wants to see in candidates on job interviews, in employees during their first few days in a new job, in more experienced professionals, and in company managers. He also speaks with authority to the growing number of women entrepreneurs, remembering his own early days in a one-man publicity office on Hollywood Boulevard.

This is a book for all young working women—for Harvard Business graduates, for recent college graduates, and for young women who are already in the work place on their way to what they hope will be a successful career. Whether your goal is simply to get a job, or to lay the foundations for a lifelong career, *Rogers' Rules for Businesswomen* can help you to achieve that goal.

Henry Rogers has supplemented his decades of experience in the work world with advice and input from successful career women in many different fields—law, banking, retailing, publishing, advertising, entertainment, consumer goods, medicine, and technology. And these women will tell you that whether your ideal working environment is corporate, creative, or entrepreneurial, certain basic rules apply to getting along (and getting ahead), so why not spare yourself years of trial and error and start playing by the rules from Day One?

It's all here: Learning more about the "hidden" job market, how and why the world of 9-to-5 is a baffling one to newcomers, understanding why your subordinates challenge your authority, how to find a mentor or two (and why you need them), what your clothes say about you and your self-image, how to survive if you think you're in over your head, key factors in starting a new business, how marriage and a family can affect your work, business travel and entertainment guidelines . . . *Rogers' Rules for Businesswomen?* Required reading!

—Abigail Van Buren
"Dear Abby"

Acknowledgments

My thanks to Michael Segalyn and Carol Hoidra for their help in the preparation of this manuscript. My gratitude also to my agent, Owen Laster, for his continuing support and encouragement.

Introduction

This book is written for women, for the hundreds of thousands or even millions of women who are about to launch or have already launched a career in the business world. This book is for you if

- you are considering pursuing a career after your college graduation.
- you are already in the business world, but you're not certain about your next steps on the way to the top.
- you are discouraged, because statistics seem to indicate that you will never get beyond a middle management position—and you want more.
- you are wondering about the trade-offs involved in having a successful career, and whether in the end the rewards outweigh the sacrifices.

My goal is to help you sort out your choices and identify your opportunities, provide some information about your concerns, and give you some guidelines for finding out about what you want, and how to get it.

You will find as we proceed through this book that there is no fixed set of rules for pursuing a career. You will learn how some successful women got to where they are, but you will also see that each one found her own way, set her own direction, followed her own path. Some women start with a company and stay with it throughout their entire working lifetime. Some women move continuously, sometimes within the same industry, sometimes changing industries, jumping in title and salary with each move they make. Some start as secretaries and work their way up to executive status. Some move straight from school into a middle management position. Some women have a one-year, two-year, or five-year plan, while others let fate take its course.

THE WORKPLACE—A WOMAN'S PLACE?

I decided to write this book because many young women have expressed to me some misgivings about their future in the business world. I have talked with students at USC, NYU, Brigham Young University, Southern Methodist University, West Virginia University, Pace University, and many other colleges and universities. Women have talked to me at Public Relations Society of America seminars and Advertising Club seminars, and at women's management groups at Southern California Edison Company, American Medical International, and numerous other companies.

I have conducted a mountain of correspondence with literally hundreds of women who have written to me ask-

ing for career advice after having read my book, *Rogers'
Rules for Success*, which was published by St. Martin's
Press in 1984. In addition, many, many women who attended a series of lectures I gave at UCLA have sought me
out for career guidance.

For four years I conducted a six-week evening course at
UCLA Extension called The Politics of Success. After each
lecture, a group of young men and women would come up
to talk with me. They would gather around—three, four,
six, or eight of them—and fire questions. I answered them
as best I could, but I was often puzzled by the differences
in the questions put to me by the women. Many of their
questions were, of course, like the young men's—"How
can I become successful?" "What is the best way to ask
the boss for a raise?" "Is an MBA really important?"—but
many of the questions asked by women were unique to
them. Their deep concern was how they could "make it" in
what they perceived as a man's world.

"Why do you think it's a man's world?" I'd ask them,
and they seemed unsure as I tried to explain to them that
the business world had changed in the last ten or twenty
years, and that today, depending on the business they
were in, it was quite likely that they were starting their
careers on an equal footing with their male peers.

Where did this concept that "it's a man's world" come
from? The fact is, it was the way things were until the
women's movement of some twenty years ago changed the
world, and women's role in the workplace, forever—and
for the better. Today, depending on the type of business
you're in and its geographical location, there may be very
little difference between the way you and your male colleagues are treated.

Statistics indicate that men are still a step above women
in salaries and in the number of top executive positions

they occupy, but that is only because women as a group have not had sufficient time to move through the "pipeline." The female account executive of today may become a vice president tomorrow, and with the world moving as steadily as it is in the direction of male-female equality, she has just as good an opportunity as her male counterparts to become president of the company fifteen or twenty years from now.

But after listening to the fears and apprehensions of many of the young women in my classes, I became concerned about the significant percentage of women who believe that their sex is a handicap, and who see the men in the office as their enemies, not their colleagues.

Where had they acquired this perspective? I heard many of them refer to books they had read in their search for advice about how to succeed in business. So I went to my local bookstore, and there they were, shelves and shelves of career advice paperbacks, all published in the seventies and early eighties. Here are excerpts from a few of them.

> For the majority of career girls, work is not a territory where they roam free, developing their strengths and their skills, but a jungle in which they are always in danger from hostile natives.
>
> —Rosalind Miles
> *Danger! Men at Work*

> It is undeniable that, in spite of all that has been done in their behalf, women still aren't achieving high positions in their careers. Many are too ready to give up before they have even climbed a quarter of the way up the ladder.
>
> —Liz Hodgkinson
> *The Working Woman's Guide*

> I dislike the militancy evoked by some feminists, but it has to be said that if we women want our share of opportunity, we must fight for it. To fight effectively, we must first recognize the enemy.
>
> —Janet W. MacDonald
> *Climbing the Ladder*

While many women are out in the workplace today, most of them are vastly underpaid and underutilized; they are doing the scrub work. They are exploited.

—Janice LaRouche
Strategies for Women at Work

In a recent Gallup Poll, 71 percent of the women surveyed said they did not have the same chance of promotions to top executive positions as did men with the same abilities.

—Marilyn Loden
Feminine Leadership

After reading these books and a number of articles that carry similar negative messages, I readily understood why many young women might wonder whether a successful career is worth all the effort that is obviously required. They may have been conditioned to believe that they are playing against bad odds.

THANKS TO THE PIONEERS

The young successful career women of today are grateful to the pioneer writers and activists who preceded them, as they should be. Lori Weintraub, an extraordinarily successful young woman in the motion picture industry, told me how she feels the success of other women before her contributed to her potential for advancement. Starting out as a hippie in the sixties, Lori suddenly decided to straighten out her life and pursue a career. She graduated from UCLA Law School, became associated with a distinguished Los Angeles law firm that specializes in entertainment law, became a production executive at MGM, a senior production executive at Lorimar Pictures, and finally President of Robert Chartoff Productions.

"I know that mine is a wonderful success story," she told me one day, "but I doubt whether I could have achieved as much in such a short time if I'd been born ten years earlier. People like Sherry Lansing, Betty Friedan, Bella Abzug, and Gloria Steinem, together with Paula Weinstein and Sue Mengers broke the ice for us who are successful today. It was comparatively easy for me, and I am grateful to all of those women who fought the battles in earlier days. Now we can all enjoy what those pioneers have given us."

WHY ME?

Because so many young women have misconceptions about today's workplace, and because I believe that there is a dearth of written material on true conditions in the workplace *today*, I decided to write this book.

The situation for career women in the United States is positive, not negative. For every negative statistic that is thrown at you, I will give you one that is upbeat and encouraging. I feel very strongly that young women should be encouraged in the pursuit of careers. Not every woman will make it, but not every man makes it either.

I have not only worked for and with women since my early youth, but women have always played important roles at Rogers & Cowan, the public relations organization that I founded. Women are more important in our company today than they have ever been before. The president of our international division is a woman. The co-head of our New York entertainment division is a woman. The president of our Washington division is a woman. The heads of our motion picture and television divisions in our Los Angeles office are women. We also have more female professionals than male in our organization. That's where Rogers & Cowan is today.

I know about the problems these women face. I know

about the unenlightened attitudes of hard-core male chauvinists, I know about restricted luncheon clubs, the infinitesimal number of women CEOs of major corporations, and all the other barriers that are placed in the path of career women. But I have been surrounded by career women all my adult life, and I also know that there are many thousands of women in today's workplace who are successfully pursuing careers. If all these women could do it, you may be able to do it too.

There are greater opportunities for you to succeed today than there have ever been before. But it's up to you. If you really want to be successful, you can be.

1

Do You Really Want a Career?

Don't say yes automatically. This is a tough question—and a key decision. Devoting your life to a career is an awesome, demanding task that calls for enormous dedication. It's easy to admire the popular media image of a career woman and say, "Oh, yes; I'm dedicated." But you won't know what having a career is really like until you get into the business world and experience the frequent frustrations, occasional humiliations, and unanticipated setbacks that are all part of the generally satisfying and rewarding career experience.

The truth is that if you pay your tuition and get passing marks you'll get a college diploma. But as you'll eventually discover, if you're not already aware, of the fact it takes a concerted effort just to stay employed in the long run. Advancement in a given field is an even greater challenge.

It's important to realize that when I write about building a career, I mean something different from having a job. Some women work from the time they graduate until they marry. Then, if they can afford it and they're not interested in working any longer, they can settle down, think about starting a family, and make home and hearth the top priority. Although you do not necessarily rule out the prospects of marriage and a family by choosing to pursue a career, once you make that choice, your top priority, main objective, and key source of satisfaction will be moving up in the business world, and getting as close to the top as you possibly can.

Do you really want a career? Ask yourself the big questions:

- Does the very prospect of success drive you to be the best you can be?
- Are leaders in the business world some of the people you admire most?
- Does a highly competitive situation make you want a prize even more?
- Do you enjoy taking on a challenge and finding new solutions?

If your answer to most of these questions is an emphatic "Yes!" this book can help you to achieve your goals.

Achieving success can take years, even decades, and it usually comes only to those who have made a conscious decision to be the best. Debbie Myers is a twenty-eight-year-old UCLA graduate who is now associated with the Interdevelopment Bank in Washington, D.C. One day I asked Debbie whether she was really devoted to having a successful career. Her reply: "My career is my life, and I'm determined to be successful." Noting that she had moved ahead steadily in her field, I asked her how she'd managed to do that. She answered, "I can sum it up in one word: perseverance. I quickly learned that it's easy to get discouraged, and I knew that if I wanted to become successful in my career, I had to stick with it, keep going, and not worry too much about making mistakes. I've had setbacks and disappointments, and although I get unhappy about them, it's only for the moment, and then I just start plugging all over again."

On another occasion I asked Barbara Corday, until recently President of Columbia Pictures Television, what advice she would give to ambitious young women who were about to enter the business world. Her observations:

- You must want success desperately.
- Remember that there are a hundred people waiting to take your job.
- Talent is only a small part of what it takes to be successful.
- In certain industries, start as a secretary if you have to.
- Don't be uppity about what you're willing to do.
- Start every day with butterflies in your stomach.
- Remember that there's always more to learn.
- Bite off a little more than you can chew—you can always learn.

ABOUT OPPORTUNITY: A CINDERELLA STORY

Do you feel that you are lacking in qualifications and opportunities? Are you discouraged because you could not afford the most expensive school, that for whatever reason you feel you are at a disadvantage because you don't "look good on paper?" Do you feel insecure because you don't have the polish or cultural background you believe is necessary for a successful career? These concerns should not prevent you from going all out for success. No one who really tries is barred from the career arena.

There are rich candidates and there are poor candidates. There are outstanding students, mediocre students, and those who barely get passing grades. There are young women who *seem* to fall into success, and those who, driven by ambition, work day and night to achieve it. There are those who graduate from law school at Harvard, Yale, or Stanford and go on to illustrious careers in the legal profession, and there are those who never even go to college—but despite even this obvious handicap, some of these people can wind up as partners in prestigious law firms.

For six years Lisa Specht has been a partner in the distinguished Century City, Los Angeles law firm of Mannatt, Phelps, Rothenberg, and Philips, and she achieved this enviable position without a BA. How did it happen?

"I don't know whether it would have happened at all if I'd been brought up in different circumstances," Lisa said. "I grew up in the claustrophobic atmosphere of La Canada, a suburb of Pasadena, and I felt that I was trapped in a life that I hated. I went to high school in Pasadena and Glendale, and I was a mediocre student. Raised in a stultifying atmosphere at home, I yearned to go away to college. But when I was seventeen I learned that my stepfather had no plans to help me financially to continue my education, and that he expected me to go to work when I graduated from high school. So I left home.

"From the ages of seventeen to twenty-five I had twenty different jobs. You name it and I did it. I was a cocktail waitress, a secretary, a receptionist, a dancer in Las Vegas and Lake Tahoe, a model . . . I finally settled down in Chicago working as an airline stewardess. After three years in Chicago, I moved back to Los Angeles.

"Up until that time, I had never thought about a career as such. I just went from job to job, not thinking that there was anything special that I wanted to do. Now for the first time, I began to think about a career. And I knew that I needed some professional advice.

"I met with Dr. Judd Marmor, a distinguished psychoanalyst. Dr. Marmor shook up my life. After we had talked for a while, he said to me, 'Lisa, you are in a position that ninety-five percent of the people in the world would love to be in. You can do *anything!*' No one had ever said anything like that to me before. I had never even thought of it."

THE TURNING POINT

"It was at that moment that I decided for the first time in my life that I wanted to make something of myself, that I wanted to be somebody.

"I got a full-time job at the ACLU [American Civil Liberties Union]. I started there as the receptionist, and in three weeks the boss asked me to be his secretary-assistant. As part of the job I worked with the Volunteer Lawyers Bureau. I found myself spending a lot of time with them, debating and arguing with them. They didn't intimidate me. I felt very comfortable with them. One day I said to myself, 'You could be a lawyer.'

"Well, I very naively started to call law schools. Naturally, they all said forget it. After all, I had never gone to college. How could I go to law school and become a lawyer if I had never gone to college? 'There must be a way,' I reasoned. There was. I called the California State Bar Association one day and learned about the college equivalency examination. If I passed that, I would be eligible to go to a law school in California, if any of them would accept me.

"It's like a Cinderella story. I got a tutor and passed the

exam. Then I talked myself into the San Fernando Valley College of Law, and I was on my way to becoming a lawyer. After four years of incredibly hard work I graduated at the top of my class, and I was editor-in-chief of the law review, the first woman ever to have achieved that position. I now had a goal, and I felt that I was really accomplishing something.

"During all this preparatory time, everyone told me that I had no chance of getting into a major law firm. I was angry, and I decided that I didn't care what they said. I remembered only what Dr. Marmor had said—that I could do anything I wanted to do. I stored up my resources, arranged to be appointed to committees, began to meet people in the political and legal arenas, and managed to get appointments for interviews with a number of major law firms. It was a special moment in my life in December of 1977 when I was offered a job with Manatt, Rothenberg, Phelps and Tunney. It was another special moment four years later when I became a partner in that firm."

The lesson to be learned is that, although education is certainly important in preparing yourself for a career, your future success is not dependent upon whether you have a high school diploma or a Harvard MBA. Many other factors, all of which will be brought to light in this book, will have a much greater impact on the degree of success you achieve than will credentials alone.

WHERE THE OPPORTUNITIES ARE

In deciding whether a career life-style is for you, you should take a look at the range of opportunities available to women today. And that doesn't mean that you should seek out only the best and ignore the worst. Just because there are only seven women numbered among the six hundred investment banking partners currently on Wall Street, that's no reason to rule out investment banking as a career for yourself. After all, 25 percent of Wall Street professionals are women, and in a few years time the number could jump to 35 percent, 40 percent, or more. If there are seven women partners today, there could be twenty-seven tomorrow—and you could be one of them.

Some fields that are currently said to offer fast-track opportunities for women include:

- Financial services
- Insurance
- Retailing
- Consumer products
- Communications
- Advertising
- Banking
- Health-care administration

Surprisingly, the new high-tech companies are also excellent career choices for women. Although traditional sex roles seldom cast women as scientists or engineers, the many women who do choose these specialties find that, in these new and rapidly growing industries, there are very few well-entrenched senior male executives who might be inclined to block their way to the top.

A few words about my own area of expertise, public relations, which falls generally under the heading of communications. At Rogers & Cowan, we are involved in corporate public relations, product promotion, sponsorship of corporate art exhibitions, and promotion of people throughout the entertainment world. A number of our women professionals are paid in excess of $100,000 a year, and many earn more than $50,000–$60,000 a year. Let me mention, too, that women are playing increasingly important roles in the motion picture and television industries. The top women in this field draw salaries of $250,000 a year—and up. Among the entertainment industry superwomen: Lucy Fisher, senior vice president at Warner Brothers; Dawn Steele, newly appointed president of Columbia Pictures; Paula Weinstein, executive production consultant at MGM; Sherry Lansing, former president of Twentieth Century Fox, presently acclaimed as the co-producer of *Fatal Attraction* with her partner Stanley Jaffe; and Suzanne de Passe, who is responsible for much of what happens in television and motion pictures at Motown these days. You should also know that the majority of top marketing, advertising, promotion, and publicity executives at *all* the leading motion picture, television, video, and cable TV companies today are women. If you are tempted to hop on a plane to Hollywood, I will not discourage you. The opportunities for women behind the silver screen, are great.

The publishing business, another communications field, also offers excellent career opportunities for women. Many, many women in this business have risen to positions at or near the top of their companies, and at least a dozen are now presidents, publishers, division heads, or even owners of their own firms.

Publishers Weekly, the leading trade publication in this industry, reported in its January 23, 1987 issue that "at least in some of the major commercial publishing houses, gender no longer carefully defines or limits one's career, and at every level from secretary to sales rep and upward from there to publisher and president, men and women are competing for the same positions."

Lynn A. Lumsden, executive vice president, publisher,

and chief operating officer of Dodd, Mead, is quoted in that same article: "It's pretty hard to find a major publishing company where women aren't in power. I mean at the level of real operating managers—financial responsibility and lots of people reporting to them."

Other powerful women executives in the publishing business agree. Sally Richardson of St. Martin's Press says, "I have never felt any sense of restriction at St. Martin's because I'm a woman. I can go as far in this company as my talent will take me."

SEX DISCRIMINATION IN THE BUSINESS WORLD

I've been telling you about the tremendous opportunities that exist for you in many areas of the business world, and citing as examples women who have made it to the top in a number of career fields. While you were reading these paragraphs, did the question, "But is there something holding women back?" cross your mind? If there are "good" fields for women, do you wonder whether there are "bad" fields? The answer to both these questions is a qualified yes.

In some occupations, or in some areas of the country, or in the eyes of some men—(one of whom may end up being your boss)—the fact that you are a woman may be perceived as a disadvantage. You may be lucky and never encounter sex discrimination throughout your entire career, or you may run smack up against it in your first job out of school.

According to an article in the January 1988 issue of *Working Woman*, women in the United States earn salaries approximately 70 percent of those of males. Only 7 percent of employed women in America work in managerial positions, and only 10 percent earn more than $20,000 a year. Male lawyers between the ages of twenty-five and thirty-four earn on an average of $27,563 a year; the figure for female lawyers is $20,573. As for retail salespersons, males average $13,002 a year while females average $7,479.

But remember that 70 percent is an average, and it doesn't mean that every woman in every job receives 30 percent less per hour than every man. More women receive as much money as their male counterparts, and in some cases even higher salaries. I happen to believe that your future is better served by looking also at some of the encouraging statistics. Take for example the results of a study conducted recently by Heidrick and Struggles, the New York–based international executive search firm, which revealed that the average annual compensation for corporate women officers of *Fortune* 1000 organizations is $116,810.

David R. Peasback, president of the firm, stated that "one in ten female executives now earns more than $200,000 a year" as against 1980, when, he explained, only 9 percent received more than $100,000. Peasback also stated that "female executives ages forty to forty-nine receive the largest paychecks, averaging $132,170 a year with almost one in ten awarded $250,000 or more.

There seems to be a difference of opinion about women's acceptability in the marketplace and the extent to which discrimination against women candidates for top management positions exist. In 1985 *Harvard Business Review* conducted a study of 1,900 male and female executives. The study revealed that since 1965 prejudices against women have diminished, but have not altogether disappeared.

In *The Wall Street Journal*'s comment on the *Harvard Business Review* survey, it was pointed out that more than half of all the respondents, both men and women, stated their opinion that women never would be wholly accepted in business. My opinion is that those who disagreed with the majority are more progressive and contemporary in their thinking and no doubt work in businesses and industries where women enjoy equal status with men.

The *Harvard Business Review* pointedly makes the observation that the single biggest change in perception in the past twenty years concerns women's desire to move up the corporate ladder. The survey reports that in 1965, fully half of the men and women surveyed agreed that women rarely expected or wanted positions of authority. In contrast, in 1985 less than 10 percent of the executives held that opinion.

My own conclusion is that as the business community becomes aware of the growing number of females holding down positions of authority, it becomes increasingly convinced that women are just as interested as men in striving for upper management positions. The good news: the opportunities for career women today are already good, and getting even better.

Rita Hauser is one of the most successful women attorneys in the United States. A senior managing partner with the prestigious firm of Stroock, Stroock & Lavan, she has an international practice and divides her working time between New York and Paris. She observes, "Law firms today are hiring as many women out of law school as they do men, but we still don't know how many of them will rise to the top. Among the law firms with which I am familiar, I do not see any sexual discrimination. You will see more men at the top, but that's for two reasons: first, there has not been sufficient time for women to go through the pipeline, and second, there are a large number of dropouts among women. The hours are grueling, the pressures are enormous, and there are certain women who finally decide that the end result isn't worth the price they have to pay for it."

Dorinda Scharf is a management consultant in the cosmetics and fragrance business. Her experience with sex discrimination: "After going through the executive management training program at Macy's in New York City I became a department manager. After nine months I was promoted to the position of assistant buyer for men's fragrances. As a young, attractive woman I was subjected to a number of snide put-down remarks by some of the men in the department, but I knew that that was part of the game, and I was determined not to be prejudiced against them. I regarded them as a challenge, and by working hard, I won their respect and finally won them over. From that point on, I never experienced sexual discrimination in that job again."

Anne Luther is vice president of public relations for Schieffelin & Co., one of the most distinguished wine distributors in the country. She says, "Sex discrimination? A lot of it is luck. It all depends on who your boss is." One of her first bosses "didn't realize that the work environment had changed in the past twenty-five years, and that, whether he liked it or not, women were a part of his world. He patronized me and the other women in the company. It was his language. He would make remarks like, 'You're doing well for a woman,' or, 'Women come cheap.'

"I never got angry with him, nor was I ever indignant. I reasoned with him. I tried to get him to understand. It was difficult for him, but I must admit that he did try."

After five years, Luther was promoted to her current

position, in which she reports to Penn Cavanagh, the chairman of Schieffelin. "It's the difference between night and day," she says. "Men and women are treated alike. He makes no distinctions, and as a result of his attitude, I can now accomplish twenty-five percent more in the same workday, because I don't have to fight the battle any longer. I don't have to justify my existence."

KEEP IT IN PERSPECTIVE

Once you become aware of sex discrimination, it is important to keep the issue, an ambiguous and highly subjective one, in perspective. Some men's personal styles and speech patterns may be profoundly annoying, until you stop and think for a moment and try to understand them. Stephanie French, a Philip Morris Company executive, told me, "When I first joined Philip Morris there were some women in our department who were sensitive about our boss at the time, who always addressed us as 'dear.' It is such an out-of-date expression, and he is an older man who has since retired. He would have been shocked if anyone had ever told him that his expression was sexist. He was brought up in an era in which women were addressed as 'dear' out of kindness and caring; it was never meant as a put-down. I explained this to the women who worked with me, and once they understood, they were never offended by him again."

Regarding this subject, a young staff reporter at a nationally-known newspaper confirmed to me that noticeable changes are taking place on the sex discrimination front. "There is none at this point in time at this particular paper. When I first joined the paper about three and a half years ago, there were very few women reporters. But there's been a big change. We now have some sixty reporters in the New York bureau, and a good forty to fifty percent of us are women."

Although sex discrimination is distinctly unfair, it is to some degree understandable. Men, who ruled the roost, fought the wars, and were the rulers of society for thousands of years, may need a little more time to fully accept women's presence on their turf, in the business world and elsewhere. To their credit, some men have already welcomed women as colleagues and subordinates, and even as managers. Younger men in particular are both willing to accept women as professional colleagues and to share household responsibilities with the women they marry. Those men who continue to discriminate against women probably also discriminate against Jews, Blacks, Asians, and anyone else whom they consider to be a threat to their supremacy in the workplace.

Faced with sex discrimination, as with any other kind of discrimination, you have several choices. Like Anne Luther, you can try to reason with the prejudiced man. Like Dorinda Scharf, you can just keep plugging and succeed in spite of the prejudice. Or, if you find yourself in a company where discrimination is prevalent, and is tolerated, and you don't want to accept the situation, I suggest that you look for another job.

Sexual discrimination is a violation of Title VII of the Civil Rights Act of 1964. Even though the law is on your side in this matter, a lawsuit is rarely a good idea, particularly if you intend to continue to work in your present field. Whether you win or lose the suit, you'll be perceived as a troublemaker, or too hot to handle. Why compromise your chances for success when you could just as easily seek out a better opportunity? The fact that every career field is a small world can work *for* you as well as against you. Your boss may well have an industry-wide reputation as a man who raises narrow-mindedness to an art form, and you'll get points for having resolved a tough situation diplomatically, while advancing your career in the process! (If you to want to know more about the law, contact the federal Equal Employment Opportunity Commission, or your State's department of labor.)

IGNORE THE PRECURSORS OF DOOM

Is the wine bottle half full, or is it half empty? That depends on the way you look at it. I suggest that you ignore the precursors of doom. Forget about the thousands, the millions of women who are out there struggling to break down the male barricades. Look instead at the women who have made it big in this so-called man's world.

Think about Mary Wells, Geraldine Stutz, Paula Meehan, Barbara Walters, Jane Pauley, Sherry Lansing, Mary Kay, and the thousands of other successful women you read about constantly in the daily newspapers and in national newsmagazines and women's magazines. There is a world out there to be conquered; if you're up to it, if you have the intelligence, the gumption, the will, and the persistence, and if you are willing to fight hard to be successful, it's all out there waiting for you.

ROGERS' RULES FOR DECIDING WHETHER TO PURSUE A CAREER

1. Realize that the odds are against your making it big—but the odds are against anyone's making it big, male or female, young or old.

2. Know that, despite the significant gains women have made in the workplace since the beginning of the feminist movement, in some jobs or some areas of the country you may still face a certain degree of sex discrimination.

3. Know in advance that, on the average, women in business earn about seventy cents for every dollar that a man earns. But ambitious women pay no attention to averages. And the odds are increasingly in your favor that you will work in a company where men and women are treated equally.

4. You may have to work twice as hard as your male colleagues to move up in the company where you're employed (if you work at that kind of company).

5. You can have a husband and children if you want them, but you should realize that they will impose additional burdens on you. (More about this in Chapter 8.)

6. You must make a conscious effort to be respected for your professional capabilities. You can't command respect; you have to earn it by doing your job well.

7. Think of your education as just beginning. Plan to learn your own job, and everyone else's as well. Your goal: to be the best prepared, most informed, most dedicated person in your company.

2

Getting Started

In choosing to pursue a career you have resolved one of the major decisions facing you at this stage of your life. Next decision: what field? If your education focused on a specific profession or skill, one might assume you'll look for a job in the field for which you were trained. If your education was not career specific, however, your options are more varied, but harder to nail down. You may consider looking for a job in advertising or banking, insurance, real estate, or even public relations, and each of those fields may hold great potential for you. But I think that too many people drift into whatever job becomes available after graduation. It's easy to think, "If I don't like this, I can always find another job." To some extent that may be true: I know lawyers who have become politicians, accountants who have become stand-up comedians, and secretaries who are now vice presidents. Your original goal will very likely change and evolve as your career progresses, and you'll have to be flexible enough to take advantage of windfall opportunities when they occur. But even starting out, it's better if you have something specific to shoot for. Drifting through a series of entry level jobs in unrelated fields, you may cover a lot of ground, but it will take you that much longer to move ahead.

FINDING OUT ABOUT "WHAT'S OUT THERE"

Your job search should begin with research into the world of opportunities that exist. When you were choosing a college and selecting a major, you probably talked to teachers, guidance counselors, and family members; you sent away for catalogues, visited campuses, compared course offerings; finally you selected a few schools to apply to that you thought fit well with your goals and aspirations. All that effort went into selecting a living and working environment for four years of your life. Don't you think that you should put at least the same effort into choosing a career, which may be your living and working environment for the next *forty* years of your life?

You have more opportunities—and more good business contacts—than you realize. You can begin by making a list of everyone you know in the business world: your parents' friends, your friends' parents, the people you baby-sit for, members of your church or synagogue, people in the companies where you've worked in the summer. Write them a letter, or call, and ask whether you might schedule a brief appointment at their convenience. Make it clear to them that you are interested in learning about the field in which they've been successful, but that you do not expect them to have a job for you, or even to know of a job. What you need now is *information*—just the facts, ma'am.

You may be shy initially about approaching these people, but let me share with you a bit of knowledge that could be helpful. Those in authority generally don't mind giving advice to younger people who seek them out. A few may be selfish and may brush you off, but for the most part you will find that people are willing to take the time to steer you onto the right track. Don't get discouraged if you are rejected by one or two so-called friends. You will find many who would welcome an opportunity to become your adviser in career matters. Prepare for these "information interviews" by finding out what you can about your contacts' companies, and about the industries in which these companies play a role. Good sources of information: the business section of your local newspaper, your parents or older siblings, and, of course, *The Wall Street Journal.*

Ask your contacts how they got to their current positions, what the growth areas in their fields are likely to be, and whether there are any other people that it might be useful for you to talk to. Take notes! Keep good records of who said what, and who referred you to whom, and always, *always* send a typed thank-you letter on 8½″ × 11″ stationery to follow up a meeting or telephone conversation.

This process of communication will help you establish relationships which will help you for years to come. It will be the beginning of your involvement with *networking,* an important activity for you to continue throughout every stage of your career. So even if you're a little shy about it at the beginning, networking is an important skill for you to master on your way to the top.

If you are fortunate enough to have influential parents or relatives, don't say to yourself, "I'm not going to ask anyone for help; I'll make it on my own." Noble sentiments, but in the harsh, competitive world that you're about to enter, they're just impractical. You must take advantage of every opportunity that will help to open doors for you. If you're not reluctant to accept help from strangers, don't let your pride prevent you from accepting a helping hand from family or friends. Because really, no one can make you successful but yourself. Your father may be able to introduce you to a friend who'll give you a job, but from the moment you walk into the office on that first day, you're on your own.

Let me give you an example. Frank Dale and I are long-time friends. We served on the same community and civic boards together during the years that he was publisher of the Los Angeles *Herald Examiner.* One day after a Los Angeles Music Center board meeting, he said to me, "I'd like you to meet my daughter."

"I'd be delighted to," I said. "What does she do?"

"She works for a public relations firm in San Francisco. She and her husband will be moving to Los Angeles in about six months, and I thought you could give her some advice."

"Of course," I replied. "I'd be glad to meet with her. Just ask her to telephone me the next time she is planning to be in Los Angeles and we'll set up a meeting." A few weeks later Holly walked into my office, and after we talked for a half hour, I decided that she had a lot to offer Rogers & Cowan. My colleagues and I agreed about Holly's capabilities. We hired her, and now, some five years later she is a vice president in our corporate division and has six account executives reporting to her, as well as office personnel.

The point is that I didn't do Frank Dale a favor when I agreed to meet with his daughter. He did me a favor, because Holly is a talented public relations executive and has proven to be one of our most valuable assets. In our business, people with Holly's attributes are difficult to find.

When Richard Zanuck decided to follow in the footsteps of his father, the late Darryl Zanuck, a legendary name in the motion picture industry, there is no doubt that the father's name was an asset to the son. But once his foot was in the door, Richard had to prove himself. Richard Zanuck is respected today as a successful movie producer whose credits include *The Sting, Cocoon, The Verdict,* and many other films you've probably seen and enjoyed. He is known today because he is responsible for producing popular, money-making films, *not* because he is the son of a famous father.

So don't hesitate to let someone you know give you an initial push. It can save you months or even years in start-up time, and in the long run your success—or lack of it—will depend on only one person: you.

In addition to activating your network of personal contacts, you should begin to familiarize yourself with general trends in the business world. You don't have to memorize the financial pages of the newspaper or read every business magazine from cover to cover, but do plan to look at the business section of your local newspaper and read the business articles in *Time* and *Newsweek.* To find information and advice directed specifically to career women, read *Savvy, Working Woman,* and other women's magazines that have a business slant. Besides learning some useful business jargon, you'll soon be able to figure out which are the growth industries. You'll have a realistic sense of the odds against you, should you find yourself attracted to a stagnant profession that is unlikely to furnish consistent opportunities for advancement. My advice: hitch your wagon to a star, not a rock.

TIME TO TALK ABOUT YOU

Now that you've done some homework and listened to a lot of people—including me—it's time to think about what *you* want. Management consultant and career development specialist Lynn Frankel of Frankel Renne Enterprises advises her clients to free-associate about their fantasy job, and to identify the individual components that make that job such a plum.

Make lists of your likes and dislikes, values and priorities, and try to assign a numerical rank to each one. Is money less important than independence? Do you just want to be the best at whatever you do? Are you a details person or a big-picture person? Also make lists of the people you like to be with, and the reasons why these relationships are so stimulating. Think about quality-of-life issues, such as whether you prefer to live and work in a city, a small town, or the wide open spaces; whether it's important for you to feel secure in your job, or if an occasional calculated risk keeps the thrill in the game; whether you're prepared to travel for business or accept a transfer to another part of the country; and whether you'd prefer a traditional corporate culture or a more freewheeling entrepreneurial situation.

Assess your strengths, weaknesses, and major accomplishments to date; for one thing, you'll be asked about them on every job interview, and it's best to appear prepared. And this exercise may keep you from making a mistake in the selection of that important first job. If you've never seen the need to balance your checkbook to the penny, chances are that any kind of job in an accounting firm would drive you crazy. And if you've always read for content rather than style, you'd be a disastrous copyeditor, although there may be other positions in the publishing industry that suit your abilities.

When you've made a composite picture of your skills—the things you like to do, the kinds of people you like to be around, and the job attributes and responsibilities that attract your interest—you'll have a much better idea of how you'd like to spend the time between nine and five. So now it's time to go after that fantasy job.

YOUR RÉSUMÉ

You probably already have a résumé that your parents or the career planning office at your school helped you to write. Now is a good time to take a long, critical look at it. Does it emphasize your strengths and accomplishments? Or is it a backward obituary of summer jobs and low-level positions that helped bring in some money but are hardly what you're in the market for now? If you knew about yourself only what is on that piece of paper, would *you* hire that person? Suggestion: get some feedback on your résumé from your first group of networking contacts. They know what they look for in a job applicant, and they may be able to help you put the good stuff up front.

What do I mean by the good stuff? If you're like most young people, you won't have wowed Wall Street or served as ambassador to the Court of Saint James'. But you may have increased the traffic to a store where you had a summer job by creating an eye-catching window display, or lined up an impressive roster of speakers for a lecture series at your college, or started a computer club in which the members discussed new developments in computer technology and swapped programs they'd written. The skills that you used to accomplish these things are skills that employers want, which you should emphasize in your résumé.

Instead of starting with an employment history listing one dull job after another, catch the reader's eye at the top of the page with a brief, well-stated career objective and list your skills and accomplishments *before* your job history and educational background. Let prospective employers know what you can do for *them*.

THE JOB HUNT

The keys to any job hunt are persistence and follow-up, and all those network referrals you've gotten are a good place to start.

You're actually much more likely to find a job with someone you know, or with someone who knows someone you know, than by answering help-wanted ads in the local newspaper. But do that, too, and go to employment agencies. And send letters to the personnel offices of the kinds of companies you think you'd like to work for. (A good librarian can point you in the right direction for corporate directories with names, addresses, and so on.) If you have a network referral to one of the decision makers in a company, write to him or her *and* to the personnel office. You'll probably get more of a reply than the polite, we-have-your-résumé-on-file letter.

There are countless examples of the ways in which persistence and follow-up have made all the difference in successful women's careers. Take the case of Sherry Lansing, former president of Twentieth Century Fox Productions, for example. A student in one of my UCLA classes asked Ms. Lansing how she'd started her career. Sherry Lansing replied that once she had decided whom she wanted to work for, she called the man *seventeen times* before he took the call and agreed to see her. That meeting led to a job, and that first job opened up an exciting and rewarding career for her.

Nobody ever said that looking for a job, especially your first job, is easy. It isn't. The whole process can be a very discouraging experience at times, but you've got to keep going, keep trying, keep moving. Every person you call and every letter you write increases the number of potential opportunities from which you'll be able to choose.

Unfortunately, the vast majority of young people who look for entry level positions go about the process in such a way that they program themselves for failure. Many times I have interviewed job applicants, asking them what they have done about finding a position before they came to meet with me. Too often, I discover that their efforts have been disorganized, lethargic, intermittent, and casual. I'm always surprised when I learn that they really believe they are doing everything they can to land a job.

If I am sufficiently interested in a person, I take the time to explain what he or she *should* be doing. After some questioning, I generally discover that the person I am trying to help puts two or three hours a day into his or her job hunt, rather than the eight to ten hours a day this all-important starting point requires. This person isn't necessarily lazy or uncaring, but it never occurs to most people that there is anything to do beyond letter writing, telephoning, and knocking on doors.

Looking for a job should be planned like a military operation. There are strategies to be developed, schemes to be devised, people to be talked to, advice to be sought. The best example I can recall about how tenacity and thoroughness can help a person land a job is the story that Jean Firstenberg told me about how she became director of the American Film Institute in Hollywood.

REALLY GOING AFTER THE JOB YOU WANT

"I was with the Markle Foundation from 1976 to 1979," Jean said, "in a responsible position. I had earned my stripes, but there was nowhere for me to go, because the president, a man I admired tremendously, had no intention of leaving. I decided to keep my eyes open for a position that would appeal to me. When I read in the newspaper one day that George Stevens, Jr. had resigned as director of the American Film Institute, I knew that that was the job for me—if I could get it.

"I knew that no one would just hand me such a plum assignment, and that if I really wanted it, I would have to campaign for it.

HOW TO START?

"I telephoned George Stevens's office at AFI headquarters in Washington and queried his secretary as to the proper procedure to apply for the position. She told me that a search committee had been selected to develop a list of candidates. She was so friendly on the telephone that I didn't hesitate to ask her for the names of those who comprised the committee. She unhesitatingly gave me the list, which I hurriedly scribbled down on my notepad. She also suggested that I send my résumé to Mr. Stevens. In studying the list, one name was familiar to me: Richard Brandt. I recalled meeting him a number of years before. I knew he was associated with the Trans-Lux Corporation, and before the day was over I had reached him on the telephone.

"He was very friendly and suggested that, before we

meet, I should send him my résumé. He must have been impressed with it, because he telephoned me a few days later and invited me to lunch. I knew that I was qualified for the job, but I was delighted to learn that Dick agreed. He told me that I was a likely candidate for the position because I had experience in the academic world, I had experience in philanthropy, I had lived in Washington and knew it well, and I came from a movie family and knew Hollywood.

"In this first conversation, Dick told me that he had decided to support my candidacy, and I was naturally glad to have him on my side. I now wanted the job desperately, even though I knew that if I got it, I would be making an unprecedented leap from my present middle management position to the top spot in an organization. I received valuable input from that first meeting with Dick, getting insights from him as to what the job entailed and what I could bring to it.

"We decided that before I talked with other members of the search committee, I should prepare for the upcoming interviews by getting in-depth briefings from people who could be helpful in supplying me with information about the available job. I met with members of the foundation community, independent filmmakers, educators, men and women I had been responsible for funding as part of my job at the Markle Foundation, and people who had a relationship with the American Film Institute.

"It was time for me to sell myself. With the complete confidence that I had gained a fund of knowledge that would get me through any interview with flying colors, I met with Gordon Stulberg. Gordon was chairman of the executive committee of AFI, and a member of the search committee. The interview was a disaster. I talked about the UCLA archives, a subject that turned him off immediately. 'We don't want any new responsibilities,' he said, 'We want our new director to take charge of the ones we already have.' The outcome of our interview was that Gordon concluded I did not appear to be a take-charge person, and I didn't seem to understand what the job responsibilities were. I was off to a flying stop.

SETBACK AND RECOVERY

"I came away from that interview devastated by my ineptness, but I had learned what to do the next time. I learned that I should follow the lead of the interviewer, talk to him about subjects that interest him, and tell him what he wants to hear. My next meeting was with George Stevens, who was resigning from the position I was applying for.

He was very reserved. I could understand it. After all, I was applying for a position that had been his for many years. I was very uncomfortable during the interview, but I learned that when you're going after a job, you should get to know everything you possibly can about the existing conditions.

"My next interview was with Jack Schneider, an AFI board member and a vice president of CBS at the time. By that time I had learned a lot. I sat for an hour and a quarter while Jack talked. I scarcely opened my mouth, but when the 'interview' was over, he told me that I was his candidate.

"My next experience was frightening. I went to Washington to meet with the other two members of the search committee, Jack Valenti, president of the Motion Picture Association, and Harry Macpherson, an attorney who had been a White House assistant during Lyndon Johnson's administration. After a few pleasantries, one of them asked, 'What is the mission of AFI?' I froze. I couldn't think of a word to say. For a moment I didn't know anything. Then God smiled on me. The words began to flow. I recited President Johnson's exact words in his proclamation that had established the AFI some thirteen years before, and I continued on to give a perfect answer to the question. Maybe God hadn't smiled on me, after all. It's more likely that the words had come back to me because I had done my homework. I won them over, and relaxed a bit—until I remembered that I still had to deal with Gordon Stulberg once again. I managed to get through a second meeting with Gordon, and then there was nothing for me to do but wait. I had done all my campaigning—or so I thought.

THE AGONY OF WAITING

"I was asked to come out to Los Angeles for a week. I learned that the search committee had boiled down the list of candidates to three, and that I was one of the finalists. They told me that this would be the last meeting. There were ten people in the room. I was bombarded with questions, and it was scary, but it wasn't over yet. They weren't finished with me. There was a second meeting, and when that was finished, they asked me to go back to my hotel room and wait. I waited for what seemed to be forever, but it was only a few hours later that George Stevens called. I had won—but the selection still required board approval before it would become official.

"Two special board meetings were called, one in New York and one in Los Angeles. I attended both of them. It was exhausting, but I got through them. There was a final vote, and then, at long last, I was confirmed as the new director of the American Film Institute. It had taken four months of campaigning from the day I had read in the newspaper that the position was open.

"I'll never forget those four months, because I learned more during that comparatively short time than I had learned during all the years of my career."

I thought Jean Firstenberg's experience might be helpful to you, even though you obviously won't be facing that kind of intensive interviewing for quite some time. Her advice:

- Do your homework! Get all the information you can about the job you're going after.
- Learn as much as you can about the circumstances in which the talent search is being conducted, and about your competition for the position.
- Learn as much as you can about the person or people who will be interviewing you. What turns them on? What turns them off?
- During your interview, just *listen* until you are asked a question. By doing this, you are certain to give the interviewer only the information that interests him or her.
- Try to find someone in the company close to the situation who can help guide you through the pitfalls of seeking this particular job.
- Be patient. The selection process often takes a long time, and you must learn to wait it out.

INTERVIEWING TIPS AND TRAPS

Even if you already have a job, you'll have to undergo another series of job interviews every time you seek a new position that will take you closer to the top of the corporate ladder. And whether or not you get that new job will depend largely on how you present yourself to your prospective employer.

Always be on time—or better yet, a little early—for an interview. Don't try your best to be on time, *be on time.* And unless you're applying for a job as a tree surgeon, wear a suit, coordinated separates, or a businesslike dress. (Perhaps you should plan to wear one of these outfits even if you're applying to be a tree surgeon.)

Be confident but not cocky, try to speak slowly and distinctly, and when the interviewer talks, *listen.* When he or she asks you questions, avoid one-word or awkwardly phrased answers. And be prepared for the killer opener: "Tell me about yourself." Despite the fact that most interviewers use this ploy all the time, it flummoxes even seasoned business people. Expect this kind of an open-ended request for information, and rehearse for it.

That's right, rehearse for it. An interview is, above all, a performance, and you can give a good one or a poor one. Taking into account the usual time demands of an interview situation (and the average person's attention span), keep your personal bio down to about two minutes. It sounds like no time at all, but time it on your watch; when it's just you talking about yourself, those 120 seconds seem to go on forever. Again, highlight your skills and accomplishments. Don't be concerned that you're just repeating the items listed on your résumé; it is sad but true that most interviewers won't have read your résumé carefully. And even if they have, it doesn't hurt to remind them of the good things you've done—and can do for them.

As an employer myself, I sit through nearly every job interview I conduct in a state of wonderment and frustration at how ineptly and unprofessionally most people handle themselves. One thought keeps coming back to me again and again: I ask myself, "Why didn't this person bone up for the interview the same way he or she crammed for exams in school? Why not spend an hour preparing for an interview? Thirty minutes?" Most women (and men) worked themselves into a state of exhaustion trying to earn an impressive grade point average, but in my experience they spend little or no time at all preparing for a job interview that could determine the course of their entire lives. It is inconceivable to me. If you get nothing more from this book, remember this bit of advice: *when going on a job interview, be prepared.*

It's so simple and so obvious, yet it is a rare and refreshing experience for me when I listen to someone who has actually prepared for a job interview. When the sons or daughters of my friends come to me seeking career advice, they don't understand what I mean when I tell them that they must be prepared for a job interview. They are rarely willing to admit their lack of comprehension, but it all comes out when I ask them to imagine that they're on a job interview with me. I ask them a few obvious questions: What experience have you had in public relations? What are your qualifications? What kind of a job are you looking for? Why do you think I should give you a job?

Invariably, as a prospective employer, I am unimpressed with, even turned off by their answers. I know that I wouldn't give them a job if they'd actually been applying for one, so I carefully explain to them where they have gone wrong. I take them back to the beginning. I show them that their lack of preparation makes it impossible for them to make a favorable impression on me, or on any other prospective boss. I then point out to them the information they should present in order to impress me. Finally, I ask them to try again, and again and again. At long last, my young friends understand what being prepared means, and they are better able to present themselves when they finally go out on an actual job interview.

The first step in preparing is to seek advice on what to

say and what not to say to your interviewer. Your networking contacts are key sources for such advice. When you've talked to several of your gurus, you may find that you have received varying opinions about how you should present yourself, how you should look, and what impression you should convey at your upcoming job interview. Then you must trust your own instincts and do what you feel is right for you. Smart strategy: put yourself in your prospective boss's shoes. If you were sitting on the other side of the desk

- what would you want to know about you?
- what would impress you about you?
- would you hire yourself on the basis of your presentation?

ACCENTUATING THE POSITIVES

My granddaughter Melissa, who is in her early twenties, and her young partner Peter came to see me one day for advice about how they should present themselves as a start-up motion picture and television production company. They started to give me their standard presentation, but I stopped them after a few minutes. "It's all wrong," I told them. "You're apologizing for your age. Your age is an asset: seventy-five percent of moviegoers today are in your age bracket. You're actually much better qualified to know what people want in movie entertainment than people who are twice your age."

They started again, and I interrupted again. "Don't tell me about your lack of production experience. That's not important right now. You're playing yourself down. Accentuate the positive. Tell me about your creativity, that Warner Brothers, New World, and Mount Productions have already optioned properties you've developed. Tell me that you are contemporary movie packagers in the tradition of The Mirisch Company, United Artists, and the Cannon Group; that you have the ability to ferret out material; that you have established relationships with agents; and that the creative talents of writers, producers, and directors are available to you. Tell me about the advantages you have, not the disadvantages. When the interviewer expresses doubt, just say, 'You're right about that, but we are confident that our advantages in this business far outweigh our disadvantages.' "

After three similar sessions, Melissa and Peter finally developed an effective presentation. They sought advice, they got it, they tailored it to their own style, and they were then well prepared to talk to and impress anyone in the motion picture industry with their qualifications.

My insights as an employer also helped Vicki Stevens, a young family friend. Vicki had just resigned from her job as a trainer for a motivational guidance organization and was now looking for new opportunities. I asked her to think of me as a prospective employer and to start talking. After a few minutes I stopped her. "Vicki," I said, "you're boring me, confusing me, and talking a lot of gobbledygook. Start all over again. Give me the high points of your career, and tell me what you're going to do for me. Remember that the person you're trying to convince isn't interested in what he can do for you. He's not a philanthropist; he wants to know what contribution you can make to his business or to his department." I met with Vicki twice, and after we had spent a few hours together, she was much better prepared to present herself to prospective employers. I was very pleased a few weeks later when Vicki called to tell me the good news—she'd just gotten a new job with a management consulting firm. "Now I know what you meant when you told me to be prepared" she said. "I bowled them over."

YOU MAY HAVE TO TAKE THE LEAD

It may surprise you, but interviews tend to be uncomfortable situations for the people on *both* sides of the desk. One thing that you should know going into the process is that the person who's interviewing you may not be very good at it. Most business people, in fact, lack polished interviewing skills, and they can neither get the best information from you nor give the best information about the position under discussion. You must be ready to pick up the ball when there is a lull in the conversation and you sense that the interviewer doesn't know what to ask you next.

But while you're talking, you must be alert to the reactions of the person on the other side of the desk. If he or she appears interested in what you're saying, you're on safe ground: keep talking. Look at the person, study him while you're talking. If his eyes begin to glaze over or wander around the room, if you sense that he isn't listening, or if he begins to fiddle with the objects on his desk, you must realize that you've lost him, momentarily, at least. Stop talking. This will get his attention. Then, instead of continuing your line of thought, ask him a question or two. This will force him back from wherever his mind had drifted. "Are there any questions you would like to ask me?" you can ask, or, "Is there anything more you would like to know about me?" Try to be sensitive to your interviewer. Maybe the interview is over. Maybe you have overstayed your welcome. Maybe he'd be grateful to you if you end the interview instead of waiting for him to call it to a halt.

What you say about yourself is probably the single most important factor in any job interview. You can literally talk yourself into a job—or right out of it. Andrea Van de Kamp was director of public affairs at Carter, Hawley, Hale, the retail company that owns the Broadway chain and many other department stores throughout the U.S., when I talked with her about her early job-hunting experiences. She is presently president of Independent Colleges of Southern California.

"When I graduated from Michigan State University," Andrea said, "I went to New York to look for a job. I really had no idea what I wanted to do, but I felt that something would come along—and it did. One day a man I knew told me that the dean of admissions at Columbia University School of Nursing was looking for a staff member to replace a woman who was leaving after twenty years on the job. I quickly arranged to meet with the dean, and I was able to sell myself to her.

"I have been asked many times how I managed to do this, with no job experience and no qualifications other than a college diploma. First, I came into the interview well prepared. I had done some preliminary research that gave me an insight into the job. And I convinced the dean that with my enthusiasm, my dedication to success, and my confidence, I could quickly acquire the specialized knowledge that was required, and that I really was better qualified for the job than anyone else. It must have been the enthusiasm and the confidence that I actually felt that convinced the dean to give me the job.

"I am fortunate that I have always had a lot of confidence in myself and I felt that I would succeed in any job I took on. In this particular case, I must have done a great selling job, because I later learned that I was the only nonnurse ever to hold a job in the admissions office of the school of nursing."

And just as important as what you *say* is what you *ask.* Remember that you're not on an interview just to answer someone else's questions. You're allowed to ask them, too, and you can set yourself above the other applicants if you pose thoughtful, relevant inquiries, for example:

- What are the responsibilities of the job?
- What are the immediate priorities for the new hire?
- What is the growth potential for the position, and the department, in the company?
- What would be the next career move from here?
- How is performance evaluated?
- How are people selected for promotion?

This line of questioning shows that you are serious about the job, and that you want to get all the information you need to hit the ground running if you're hired. (Again, remember to send a follow-up letter to your interviewer thanking him or her for time spent with you and restating your interest in the job.)

ROGERS' RULES FOR JOB INTERVIEWS

1. Practice for interviews with business acquaintances who can give you good advice about selling yourself to prospective employers.
2. Study the companies at which you are interviewing. Look up the back issues of that particular business's leading trade press journal. Become knowledgeable about changes that have taken place in the company, its strategy, its sales, its marketing and advertising policies, and any important changes in top personnel.

3. Be alert to the chemistry between you and your interviewer, and adjust your remarks accordingly. Is he or she cold and formal or warm and friendly, impatient or relaxed?
4. Understand which of your accomplishments might mean the most to your interviewer, and talk about the most important of these first.
5. Speak precisely, know your facts, and try to anticipate the questions you'll be asked. If they aren't asked and you feel that your prepared answers are relevant, ask the questions yourself. Say, "You may want to know that . . ."
6. Try to develop the interview into a dialogue in which you will be asking pertinent questions as well as answering them. Your questions should indicate your knowledge of the company.
7. If you are currently employed, mention the company you work for, and explain why you are interested in the new position you are discussing.
8. Never, never say anything disparaging about your present boss or the company you work for. If you do, the interviewer will probably assume that someday you will talk about him or her in the same way.
9. Promptly follow up any interview with a thank-you letter and a telephone call.

"OH, NO—NOT A SECRETARY!"

What do you do when you just can't get the job you want? You have to settle for less—sometimes for a lot less. Finally, in desperation, a horrible thought occurs to you. "My God," you say, "I'll just have to get a job as a secretary! What a terrible thought!"

You start talking to yourself, "Why did I waste all those years in school educating myself? If I thought I'd end up like this, I wouldn't have bothered going to college. I could have become a secretary five years ago. What happened to those grand ideas I had of having a successful career? I'm just washed up."

If your job search is temporarily stalled and you've begun to talk to yourself in those terms, *stop*. You're all wrong. Starting as a secretary can be the first step in launching a highly successful career.

Before you decide to accept a secretarial position, however, make sure it's regarded as a standard entry level job for both men and women in your chosen field. If your ultimate goal is to be an investment banker, you'd be better off applying for a position in a training program. But it's normal for aspiring television producers to begin their careers as production secretaries. At the William Morris Agency, one of the largest theatrical and literary agencies in the world, a large percentage of the successful male agents started in the mail room and moved up to secretarial positions; eventually, if they showed promise, they were introduced to agenting. I have had three male secretary-assistants in recent years. One now runs his own publicity firm, another left us to join a competitive public relations firm as an account executive, and the third remains with our company in an important capacity.

MANY, MANY SUCCESS STORIES

Isobel Silden started her career as my secretary at Rogers & Cowan many years ago. She has moved up to become a highly paid account executive, and she finally retired to a less pressure-filled life as a freelance writer, from which she still derives a very substantial annual income. Lois Smith, one of the most prestigious public relations women in New York, also started her career as my secretary. And Pat Kingsley, head of PMK, another high-powered entertainment public relations firm, started her life in the business world as Warren Cowan's secretary. Lynn Nesbit, senior vice president of International Creative Management, the talent and literary agency, began her career as a receptionist for the Sterling Lord Agency. Today she handles such clients as Tom Wolfe, Michael Crichton, Adam Smith, Michael Korda, and numerous other successful literary figures.

JoAnn Manley, presently group vice president of Time, Inc., started as a secretary and recommends it as a way of getting in on the ground floor. "Starting as a secretary," she says, is a shrewd course for any ambitious young woman. It plugs you into higher levels than most junior positions."

Terrie Williams, vice president of public relations at Essence Communications, says, "Our organization is a perfect example of the established fact that a secretarial position can be a perfect launching platform for a successful career. In our company there are thirty women who are nonsecretaries, and among these thirty, ten started as secretaries. They now hold such positions as poetry editor, assistant editor, director of reader services, and production coordinator in our business division."

There is no greater partisan of using the secretarial route as a way to launch a career than Kathie Berlin, presently a television producer with Thomas, Hart & Berlin Productions in New York. "I started as a secretary at WNEW-TV in New York," Kathie Berlin told me one day. "I went to work for the TV shows *Wonderama* and *The New Yorkers.* I lined up interviews, and publicists called me up all the time, pitching people to be interviewed on the shows. Because our offices were understaffed, I learned about production and public relations. Then United Artists hired me as a publicist. Four years later, I moved to MGM and stayed there until the company closed its New York City office. While on a freelance assignment, a book promotion tour for Gina Lollobrigida, the publicists Rogers & Cowan invited me to join them. I rose from publicist to president of their New York Division.

"The important thing to remember," Kathie continued, "is that before you can start building a career, you must get your foot in the door—somewhere, somehow. You should certainly begin by looking for a job that appeals to you. But don't be disappointed if you don't get it. The job you dote on today may be of no interest to you tomorrow. Many friends of mine studied law for years and finally got their degrees. But once they began to practice law, it bored them and they left the profession to do other things.

"If you can't get a job doing something that really interests you, then learn secretarial skills and become a really good secretary. Talented secretaries are always in demand because there are so few of them, and a secretarial position is the best possible door-opener to any profession that interests you."

Marcia Nasatir has had an illustrious career in the motion picture industry as a literary agent, an assistant editor at Dell Books, a vice president at Orion Pictures, and as a motion picture producer. Marcia says, "If you're looking for a career in this business [motion pictures] and you're starting as a secretary, work for a company where you would like to have a career. Accessibility is the key. Take a job doing anything in the business you want to work in. Find out what skills you have that would be useful in the business and learn the ones you don't have."

Jacqueline Byrne, district manager of the corporate advertising department at AT&T in New York, graduated from high school and went to work at AT&T as a secretary. Here is what Jackie has to say: "I don't know whether I would have been willing to start as a secretary if I'd graduated from college before I got my first job. In my case I had no choice, because I went to work right out of high school. I worked myself up from the secretarial ranks at AT&T to my present position. I am a well-paid middle manager, and I'm well satisfied with the progress I've made over the years."

COLLEGE GRADS DO IT, TOO

Steffi Atherton is senior vice president of administration of one of the most prestigious advertising agencies in the United States. She says, "I graduated from a small college in Pennsylvania. I had majored in English and had a choice of becoming a teacher or a secretary. Those seemed to be the only two choices I had in those days. I couldn't see myself as a teacher, so I took the secretarial route by enrolling in Katherine Gibbs Secretarial School. I don't know the status of Katherine Gibbs today, but I still practice the skills every day that I learned when I was a student there.

"I have many young women come to me for advice," she continued. "And unless they have trained themselves for a particular profession, I advise each one of them to start as a secretary. Once you get the door open, then it is up to you to develop opportunities for yourself."

ROGERS' RULES FOR GETTING THE JOB YOU REALLY WANT

1. If you can, make friends with your prospective employer's secretary. Secretaries and other support people can be a very important part of your network.

Why? They may be able to influence the boss to grant you an interview. They can also give you valuable advice about how to handle the interview if you are fortunate enough to get one.

2. Enlarge your list of job prospects. Most young women who are out job-hunting cover only a small part of the field. Look in the yellow pages under the categories of the businesses you are interested in, but don't write letters cold. Call the president's secretary, tell her what kind of job you're looking for, and ask her the name and title of the person to whom you should address your initial inquiry. You should also canvas the employment agencies in your city and the help-wanted ads in the classified section of your local newspaper.

3. Study and contact the executive search firms in your city. This may sound strange to you, because executive search firms work for companies, they don't act as employment agencies for individuals. However, if you can get the name of a specific executive recruiter in the firm, write and suggest that one of the firm's clients might need a capable assistant, and you would like the opportunity to meet and try to convince him that you are worthy of his recommendation.

An aside here: many young women have asked me, "But won't people think I'm too aggressive?" They might, but I would rather have them think of you as too aggressive and be aware of your presence than have them not even know that you exist. And chances are that they *won't* think you're too aggressive. It's much more likely that they will admire the fact that you were smart enough to seek their attention.

4. Be persistent. I've written this before, and I'll write it again and again, because it is the most important quality to have in looking for a job. Don't call a person once or twice and then get discouraged because he

has not returned your call. Call him five, ten, twenty times—two or three times a day, in fact, day after day. In most cases you will eventually get a call back, even if it's from his secretary, telling you that he's not interested. At least you can then cross that name off your list and go on to the next one. Are you making a pest of yourself? Maybe—but don't worry about it. Your only interest is to get the door open, and if you make a pest of yourself in the process, so be it.

5. Think of new and different approaches to get to the person you want to see. One day I dropped in to see a business executive friend of mine. There was a long-stemmed rose on his desk. I asked him about it and he replied, "Some young lady has been calling me every day asking for an appointment, but I just haven't bothered to take her calls. Today she sent me this rose, and I was so impressed with her ingenuity and persistence that I've agreed to see her."

You never know what will impress the person you're trying to see, so try everything you can think of to attract his or her attention. Send a Mailgram, send a birthday card if you can discover his or her date of birth. Send holiday greetings, or send a long-stemmed rose. It might impress your prospective interviewer as much as it impressed my friend.

3

Making the Transition to Nine-to-Five

Proudly armed with a new undergraduate degree, or even a graduate degree, some young people enter the business world with the belief that their education has prepared them for a career. They may believe that they will quickly adjust to life in the workplace, and that the many thousands of dollars spent on their education ensure that an interesting position awaits them in the real world. That is not necessarily true if you majored in a liberal arts discipline or in other subjects that do not provide career-specific training.

I am reminded of an eye-opening experience I had a few years ago that illustrates my point. A friend of mine asked me to meet with a young woman who had just completed graduate study in communications at one of the top schools of its kind in the country.

The young woman and I started to chat. She was attractive, intelligent, and personable. My immediate reaction was that she would have no problem in launching herself in a successful career in some area of the communications field. I began to question her about areas of communications with which I have some familiarity.

"What did you learn about public relations?" I asked.

There was a pause. She thought for a moment. "I guess I didn't learn anything about public relations," she replied.

I tried again. "Advertising?"

"No, nothing," came the reply.

"Broadcasting?"

"No."

"Satellite transmission?"

"N-no-oo . . ."

"Telemarketing?"

"Absolutely not."

Finally I ran out of communications businesses about which I thought she might have been knowledgeable. Frustrated with the answers I had received, I posed one more question.

"Then what did you learn at school?"

This time there was no hesitation in her reply. "I learned theory," she responded.

Those of you who have had the best educations our country can offer may, at some point, discover that you nonetheless seem to lack the practical skills needed to enter the business world. Now is the time for you to get an indication of what you can expect. It is difficult for you to anticipate what lies ahead. What should you do? What should you not do? How should you act? Should you take risks or should you play it safe? Should you seek advice or should you brave it out on your own? How should you act with your co-workers? Your boss? Will people like you or dislike you? Does it matter?

These and a thousand other questions are in your mind right now, and if they aren't, they should be. Women don't become successful just by chance, by luck. Sure, you can get a lucky break and land a cushy job without much effort, but how long will you keep it, and what should you do to eventually move from that job to a better one?

To get your career started in the right direction, and to keep it on course in the years to come, there are certain rules of thumb that you should know. In the following pages you will find out about some of these practical guidelines, which I advise you to keep in mind for both present and future reference.

YOUR EDUCATION IS JUST BEGINNING

Whether you graduated from a junior college in North Dakota or received an MBA from Harvard, you must realize that your education will really begin when you make the transition from college to the world of nine-to-five, and that the education process will continue throughout your business life.

Fran Curtis majored in public relations at Boston University School of Communications. She learned the basics of the field there, and she came to work for us some twelve years ago. She is presently one of our most successful and highest-paid executives, but she confessed to me one day, "I learned more in one year at Rogers & Cowan about public relations and the business world than I did in all the years I spent in school."

Some of the character traits that guided you successfully through your academic career—curiosity, perseverance, integrity—will serve you well in business. But the differences between school and this brave new world are in many ways more striking than the similarities. Perhaps the fundamental difference between the business world and academe is that you no longer get points just for showing up for the lectures. Business is about *money*, mostly other people's money, and those people do not have a lot of patience with anyone who's just along for the ride.

Although working in the business world is a fascinating, lifelong learning experience, its primary function is *not* to provide you with an entertaining educational opportunity. Your responsibility now is to render competent service to the organization that issues your salary check. Or, as it's sometimes bluntly phrased, "That's why they call it work."

When you take on the responsibilities of a full-time, career-path job, the consequences of your actions suddenly become more serious. A mistake in arithmetic that one of your teachers would just have corrected with a sigh could cost your company money. Simply forgetting to return a telephone call could lose an important client. We all make mistakes, of course; it's inevitable. But an error in judgment is different from thoughtlessness or carelessness, two trivial sins that no serious business person can afford to indulge in. If, as Barbara Corday advises you "start every day with butterflies in your stomach," and you are anxious to do well, how will you know how you're doing? In business, there are no midterms or finals, and if your boss is not the type to drop by occasionally and say, "You did a good job on that year-to-date sales analysis," you may not know from week to week whether you're a superstar or a potential washout.

After being accustomed to the regular rewards of seeing your list of A-pluses at the end of each semester, you may find the longer-term "grading system" of business difficult to get used to. In many companies, the annual performance review is the forum for feedback on employees' performance and progress on the job. Generally, the review is a one-on-one meeting of about a half hour between you and your immediate superior, in which he or she discusses with you your accomplishments, the areas in which improvement could be made, and your prospects for the forthcoming year. If appropriate in your case, raises, bonuses, and promotions may be discussed in this meeting—and these are the A-pluses of the business world.

If you work for a company that holds annual or semiannual performance reviews with employees, you may consider yourself fortunate. Why fortunate? Because at least someone is keeping score, and you always know how you are regarded by your employer. However, in many smaller organizations, the relationship between management and staff may be less formal, and you'll never know your performance score until one day you get a raise—or a dismissal notice. Because you are not about to change company policy—at least, not at this early stage of your career—I suggest that if you find yourself working in a company like this, you ask your boss for informal performance reviews, possibly as frequently as every three months.

How will you know what is the proper time to approach him about this? Study his work habits. When is he comparatively at ease, and under the least amount of pressure? In the early morning when he is having his first cup of coffee? After lunch, just before he gets into his afternoon work load? At the end of the day, just before he leaves for home? And what do you say to him once you determine the proper moment to talk with him? Try this.

"I would like your advice, and I'd appreciate it if you could give me a few minutes of your time. [Bosses like to be asked for advice.] I want to move ahead in this company. I've been in this job for three months now, and I'm very anxious to know how you think I've been doing."

I'll bet I can tell you what his response will most likely be. He'll say, "You're doing just fine." Don't accept that for an answer. He gave it too quickly, without even thinking. Don't let him off the hook. Have a string of questions ready for him, and ask them one by one, waiting for his answer before proceeding to the next one. Here are some questions you might consider asking:

- Am I working up to your expectations for me?
- Are we in agreement about what my priorities are?
- Is there anything you would like me to do that I have not been doing?
- Am I communicating with you satisfactorily, or is there room for improvement?
- Do you mind if we have this conversation again three to six months from now?

If he answers your questions truthfully, and he probably will, you will have just received your first evaluation, and you'll know exactly what you have to do to improve your performance.

GIVE SOME THOUGHT TO WHERE YOU'LL GO FROM HERE

You must learn the business you're in. I'm not referring to learning your own job; that's a given. But envision your company as a ladder, with you standing on the bottom rung. The second rung is the job of the person who's just above you, the next rung represents the person just above him or her, and so on all the way up to the chairman of the company. Now you can see what your long-range objective must be. Eventually you may have to learn *everyone*'s job. But don't concern yourself with such an objective just now. Let's look instead at the immediate future. Learn your own job as well as you or anyone else could possibly know it. Then begin to look at the job of the man or woman who is just above you in the organization.

Why? Because if you are to move up in the company, it is most likely that you will be moved up to the next position—*if* you perform well in your first job and *when* that position above you opens up. It will be to your advantage if you already know a great deal about that position when it becomes available. So you should begin to study the person who holds that job, and become familiar with what he or she does. Try to become friendly with the person. The closer you can get, the easier it will be for you to ask questions, understand the job, and know what it takes to do it. You're not necessarily trying to shove your superior aside, you simply want to be sufficiently qualified should an opportunity for advancement arise at your company or another. Furthermore, you were hired to assist your boss, and the more you know about your boss's goals the better you'll be able to help achieve those goals. Should the person *know* that you are trying to learn about his or her job? That depends. If he or she is friendly, outgoing, and appears to be helpful to others, you are probably safe in admitting that you hope to make a career in that field and that you want to learn. However, if he or she is an unpleasant person, cold, hostile, and fiercely protective of his or her turf, then don't expect a warm reception, and try to learn discreetly, i.e., without making your boss feel threatened.

PATIENCE, PATIENCE

You're not going to become a success overnight. In fact, it may take a year or more before you move beyond your first entry level position. Are you startled by the thought of spending a whole year, or two or three, doing the same job? As you are probably beginning to realize, building a successful career is a long-term commitment, and it involves paying a certain amount of dues at the beginning. You pay your dues when you work industriously at an entry level position for a year or more—and perform with good grace all the annoying little tasks that make you wonder, "Is this what I went to college for?" Taking the long view, you know that this first job is a means to an end, a stepping-stone. Every skill that you master and every little area of the business that you learn about makes you a little bit better than you were before, and takes you one step closer to your goal: the top.

Iris Dugow, prominent Hollywood television production executive, has said that you'll have to work twice as hard as a man in order to become successful. But Barbara Corday, a successful television executive, doesn't agree. She says that the competition is so tough that you'll have to work twice as hard as *everyone* if you really want to stand out from the crowd. Helen Gurley Brown notes in her bestselling book *Having It All* that a certain amount of drudge work must be expected in the early years of your career. She writes:

> There is no way to succeed and have the lovely spoils—money, recognition, deep satisfaction in your work—except to put in the hours, do the drudgery. If you give, you get. If you work hard, the hard work rewards you. Restless young people (you?) tend to think other people do it some other way than through slaving for it—that others are not only luckier and cleverer but that "it" somehow just falls on them and, presto, they're in the "big time." Almost *never* does that hap-

pen. Nearly every glamorous, wealthy, successful career woman you might envy *now* started as some kind of schlep.

Diane von Furstenberg used to lug a bunch of sample dresses around in heavy suitcases to stores when nobody wanted her *or* her dresses. Julia Phillips, Academy-Award-winning producer of *The Sting* and *Close Encounters of the Third Kind*, was once a novice fiction reader at the *Ladies' Home Journal*. Gloria Steinem, pretty enough to go through life as a goddess, got a job as a Playboy bunny, wrote about her experience, and kept writing until she became an editor of *Glamour* and *New York* magazines, then became a leading figure in one of the most important revolutionary movements of our lifetime—the women's liberation movement.

PUTTING IN THE HOURS

It is almost academic to state that one of the first rules of thumb you should be aware of is that successful women, and those women who are moving up quickly, put in the hours. There are very few instances—in fact, none that I can think of—of successful women who think of work as a nine-to-five affair. When circumstances warrant it, the high-powered women executives that I know remain at their desks for an hour or two after everyone else leaves in the evening; they carry briefcases filled with work home with them and put in more hours over weekends if they feel it is necessary.

All of this is applicable to you if you care enough, if you are ambitious enough. I recall one of the writers in our office who always kept a clock on her desk. Precisely at the stroke of five she would get her things together, and in thirty seconds she was out the door. One of my associates passed by her office as she was getting ready to leave and noticed that a sheet of paper was still in her typewriter. He dropped by my office, told me what he'd just seen, and said, "I wonder what she does when she's in the middle of a sentence."

You should not consider all those hours I'm referring to

as just hard work. The pursuit of a career is exhilarating, gratifying, and sometimes frustrating and aggravating; it should never be considered merely hard work. I hope that you really enjoy your job and other jobs you will have as your career progresses. And if you do, I hope you will adopt my attitude: I never work *hard*—working hard is what prisoners on a chain gang do—I just work *long*, and I love it.

INTRO TO STIFF UPPER LIP

One of the early lessons for you to learn in this postgraduate education program you are just beginning is that there is an enormous difference between accepted college or university behavior and accepted business world behavior. In school You could laugh or cry, sing or dance, lose your temper, use four-letter words, and behave outrageously if you and your friends were so inclined. In the business world it is very different. First of all, your behavior is under constant scrutiny, and whether anyone will admit it to you or not, you will be judged and evaluated as much on your behavior and professional demeanor as you will on your performance on the job. Professional behavior frequently goes against the grain of what seems natural, but it is an important part of an orderly business environment, and it is essential to your progress in that environment.

Because you are a young woman just beginning your career, your colleagues and superiors may have certain assumptions about the way you are likely to behave in the workplace. These discerning individuals may base their assumptions in large part on society's prevailing, if wrongheaded, male and female myths. "That's not fair," you protest, and you're right. But contrary to the law of the land, when it comes to sexual stereotypes we're all guilty until proven innocent.

For example, emotional outbursts disrupt work and ultimately decrease productivity, and they are condemned by both male and female bosses. Judith Price, publisher of *Avenue Magazine* in New York, has posted a sign: CRYING IS NOT PERMITTED IN THIS OFFICE. Crying and uncontrollable displays of temper are considered to be the ultimate transgressions for businessmen and businesswomen. They cost one credibility as a professional. They affect for the worse how you are perceived by your peers, your subordinates, and your boss. Tears and violent outbursts are associated with weakness, and if weakness does exist, it should be hidden. As difficult as it might be at the time such feelings are aroused, it's important to keep extremes of emotion to yourself. The next time someone in your office drives you to a state of potential frenzy, and you're either going to burst into tears or commit murder, try out the power reaction: complete silence for a second or two, followed by perfect, if distant, courtesy. Your opponent will take you for a professional diplomat, and you may end up on the boss's team of ace negotiators.

CAN YOU REALLY DRESS FOR SUCCESS?

In these early days of your career, you are probably asking yourself, "What shall I wear?" This is not a question to treat lightly. It will continue to be an issue throughout your business life, so it makes sense to deal with a few basics now.

Can you really dress for success? The short answer to this question is no, but you can certainly dress for failure.

Despite the best efforts of women's fashion magazines to convince us that women are now free to look sexy and feminine at the office, they really can't. (It might be wise to remember that what keeps these magazines in business is advertising revenues from fashion manufacturers.) Take a look at the day to day turnout of most top women executives in this country, and you'll still see a lot of suits. Particularly in the corporate world, if you want to get ahead, you play by the rules of the team, and you wear the team uniform. Period.

It may seem odd to you as a woman, but looking "too feminine" can be the kiss of death in the business world. "How ridiculous," you say. "I'd never discriminate against a man for looking 'too masculine.'" No, you probably wouldn't, and neither would most men. But, as I stated earlier, in the majority of business situations today, men are still calling the shots, even when it comes down to setting the standards of appropriate office attire.

A young woman friend of mine says, "Beware the cute little dress. Why should a financial wizard or a marketing genius even *want* to look like Little Orphan Annie?" The tiny flower prints, lace collars, and puffy sleeves of what my friend calls "the cute little dress" make women look like little girls, and no one would send a little girl to do a man's—or a woman's—job. The frailty, passivity, and childishness that this kind of attire calls to mind would compromise the credibility of a woman who was number one in her corporate raider class at Harvard Business School. Just imagine your father or your husband setting off to work in short trousers and a Cub Scout cap, and you'll have some idea of the effect of the cute little dress on the businessman's psyche.

Equally inappropriate in most offices are skirts that are too short, too tight, or slit up to here; revealing blouses;

tight sweaters; spike heels, etc. Not only is this style of dressing potentially damaging to your credibility as a professional, it also broadcasts signals that are likely to bring you the wrong kind of attention (see Chapter 7).

Although the finer points of office style are governed by your industry, your position, your budget, and the area of the country in which you live and work, you will generally not make a mistake if you wear a suit, coordinated jacket and skirt, or dress and jacket. Smart strategy: dress for the job you *want*, rather than the job you have.

I thought you might be interested to know what some of my women friends have to say about working wardrobes.

Barbara Corday, former president of Columbia Pictures Television, has interesting insights into dressing the part. Barbara started her career as a television writer. "In our business," she said, "television writers, men and women alike, dress as if they're going to a baseball game. When I went to ABC-TV in my first executive position, I found that all the men were wearing suits and ties, and I knew then that I had to dress accordingly. I bought executive-type clothes. First suits, then dresses or separates that I felt were right for my position. I adopted the uniform of the building. When I achieved my present position in our company, I started to dress down again. Unless I am scheduled for a corporate meeting or another important appointment that day, I'm back to sweaters and skirts again. Why? I guess I made the change because of the added confidence I've gained in myself, and because once you've achieved a certain position, you can make your own rules, providing they're not too outrageous."

Patty Matson, a corporate executive at Cap Cities–ABC in New York, observes, "People make superficial judgments about you before they know you, so you can't take chances. Silk blouses, skirts, and suits carry anybody through, all the time. When I arrived in New York from Washington I decided that I needed a whole new wardrobe. I went to a store and bought five silk blouses, six skirts, and two suits. These clothes lasted me for a whole year."

I have asked other women friends who enjoy successful careers for their dos and don'ts for business dressing. From their observations and my own experiences I have prepared a list of guidelines that may prove helpful to you.

ROGERS' AND HIS FEMALE FRIENDS' RULES FOR BUSINESS DRESSING

1. Avoid tight skirts and low-cut blouses.
2. Don't wear slit skirts; they're too provocative.
3. Don't take your shoes off in the office; it's unbecoming.
4. Dresses, suits, and separates are all appropriate, depending on the nature of your work.
5. The "little girl" look is out. Forget it.
6. Skirts should be pleated or flared sufficiently to permit you a free stride.
7. Don't try to outdress women who are in positions superior to yours.
8. Don't wear distracting accessories. Stay away from anything that wiggles, jiggles, or jangles.
8. Makeup should be natural-looking, not excessive. (And if your hair or makeup needs a touch-up, do it in private.)

UNDERSTANDING AND SPEAKING SHOPTALK

If you want to win the respect of your co-workers, you must become familiar with subjects of interest to them. Politics, world affairs, and the economy are obvious choices, and you can become conversant on these subjects by reading your daily newspaper and newsmagazines, or by watching the news on television. The one thing, though, that will make you really stand out among your colleagues is your ability to participate in *shoptalk*. Shoptalk is the language that your co-workers speak when they discuss the business in which you're all involved.

A different language is spoken in virtually every industry within the scope of U.S. business. If you walk into the commissary at Apple Computer at lunchtime, it may be difficult for you to understand what everyone is talking about. With no previous business experience, it would be equally bewildering for you to sit in on meetings at Lockheed, J. Walter Thompson, Bell Laboratories, or Time, Inc. Each of these businesses has its own distinctive jargon, key issues, and corporate culture.

Supreme Court justices talk about law when they are among their own, and most people talk about their businesses, especially when they are in a work environment. During the working day—and frequently far into the night—Wall Streeters talk about the stock market, mergers, acquisitions, arbitrage, and junk bonds. Marketing people talk about the Coke vs. Pepsi "war," and advertising executives spend their lunch hours discussing the Saatchi & Saatchi expansion in the U.S. and the newly announced Procter & Gamble advertising budget. In every office throughout the country, every day, five days a week, the talk is mostly work, work, work, job, job, job, business, business, business. If you're smart, you'll use this daily exchange as a stage to spotlight your abilities and insights.

How do you do this? Take on the following assignment, which really isn't difficult.

ROGERS' RULES FOR TALKING SHOP WITH THE BEST OF THEM

1. To play the shoptalk game, start by listening. Listen to the language, the vocabulary. It's familiar to you because it involves your business, your job.
2. Read the trade publications that report the news and issues of your particular business.
3. Read the daily papers and magazines in which special sections, pages, and columns cover subjects of interest to people in your industry.
4. Don't hesitate to ask your colleagues for their opinions on events that occur in the course of doing business, new government regulatory issues that may affect your industry, etc.
5. Once you have a good understanding of the issues and a new fluency in your business's buzz words, jump in! You have everything to gain, and only your anonymity to lose.

4

Your First Day on the New Job, and Beyond

The moment you walk into the office on that fateful first day, you are being sized up. Whether you are a boss, a middle manager, or a mere foot soldier at the bottom of the corporate hierarchy, you are being judged by everyone with whom you come in contact. The reactions you get may be positive, negative, or neutral, but remember that *you* are responsible for the impressions you make.

It is important that you make a favorable first impression, because first impressions are often lasting impressions. It isn't fair, and it may not even be particularly intelligent, but people *do* judge books by their covers, and your co-workers will remember you as they saw you on that first day. I'm sure that you recall conversations when you were in school when someone would say, "Do you remember what she looked like that first day in class? That terrible dress she was wearing, and her hair was a mess!" You probably remember someone else saying, "I liked her the first minute I saw her. She looked a little frightened meeting us all for the first time, but she was warm, friendly, and outgoing, and I just knew that I was going to get along with her."

In business, the first impression you make lays the foundation for the kind of relationship you will have with your boss and your co-workers. It will influence their decisions about whether they should take you seriously, whether you will be a threat, whether or not you'll fit in with the group, and whether or not they'll like and respect you during the time you'll all be working together.

If you are as thoughtful as I hope you are, you will ask me, "But why is it so important that these people like and respect me? Isn't my success dependent on my own talents and abilities?" Here's a surprise for you—the answer is no. Your success depends not only on your talents and abilities, but also on how you are perceived by others. I will have much more to say on this subject later on, but in the meantime, keep this rule of thumb in the back of your mind: your success is partially dependent on the way you are perceived by your boss and your colleagues.

THE COMPONENTS OF A GOOD FIRST IMPRESSION

I dealt with the subject of clothes in the previous chapter, but the impression you create your first day on the new job is so important that I'll raise the subject once more.

The very first thing people notice about you, before you even open your mouth to say good morning, is what you are wearing. If you were previously interviewed for your job within the office, you had an ideal opportunity to look carefully at what the other employees consider appropriate office attire. You should use your observations as guidelines for your nine-to-five wardrobe. If the company dress code calls for a T-shirt, blue jeans, and running shoes, then that is what you should turn up in. If, on the other hand, suits and silk blouses are the order of the day, then that is what you should take out of your closet the morning of that first day.

I assume that you will pay attention to the other details that make up your outward appearance: hair, fingernails, stockings (no patterns—and no runs), makeup (natural-looking), and jewelry (tasteful, and not too much).

I cannot overemphasize just how sensitive entrenched employees are to a newcomer. The other day a temporary secretary in our office was told not to come back the second day because she was wearing one long dangling earring. When I asked why we had been so harsh on the young woman, I was told that the earring indicated a lack of sound business judgment on her part, which would reveal itself time and time again if she were to remain in our organization on even a temporary basis. I'm not passing judgment on the decision, I'm just trying to impress on you the importance of your outward appearance, particularly on that first day.

Now that we have dealt with your personal appearance, it is important to consider the ways in which your behavior that first day may affect the impression you make on your boss and your co-workers. The following Rogers' Rules, if you follow them, will help to insure that from the moment you step onto the fast track you'll be putting your best foot forward.

ROGERS' RULES FOR GREAT FIRST-DAY IMPRESSIONS

1. If your boss doesn't take you around to introduce you to everyone in your department—which he or she should do—try to get someone else to do it. The obvious candidate is the boss's secretary. (If *you* are the boss's secretary, then ask the secretary at the next desk to help you out. It is unlikely that she will refuse.)
2. Smile as you are introduced. Look each person in the eye, shake hands, and tell your co-workers how pleased you are to be with the organization. Don't be reluctant to speak up. If you behave like a mouse that first day, you'll be eating cheese forever.
3. Don't smoke at your desk. In view of society's current attitude toward smoking, you are likely to offend at least some of your associates. If you wish to smoke a cigarette, do it in the designated smoking area of the building.
4. Don't chew gum in the office. It's fine for high school kids, but it is considered ill-mannered and immature in an office environment.
5. If and when it's time for a coffee break, don't hang back. Join the others, introduce yourself to those you haven't met, and enter into the conversation.
6. Do the same during the lunch hour. If your company has a cafeteria or a commissary, get your lunch, and carry your tray to a table where people who appear to be friendly, are seated. Introduce yourself. Say something like, "May I join you? This is my first day." Your touch of humility almost assures you of a warm welcome.
7. As for your boss, when you first arrive, ask him if he has anything specific he wants to discuss with you

before you start working. Be pleasant and try not to appear too nervous.

8. Study your boss throughout the day. Your career at this moment in time is, to a very large degree, dependent on how he reacts to you, and it's important for you to get to know his personal and work habits as quickly as possible.

9. As your boss is about to leave at the end of the day, stop him for a moment. Tell him how pleased you are to be working for him, and that you hope he will be pleased with the way you handle your job.

10. Unless he specifically asks you to go home because he plans to work late, stay until after he leaves. This will certainly make a favorable impression on him.

BUILDING ON THAT FAVORABLE FIRST IMPRESSION

You're off to a good start. What's next? I'm going to assume that you are a woman of average or better than average talent, so I believe that the keys to your future success include your behavior, your ability to relate to the people around you, and your ability to sell yourself to them.

If you are going to succeed in your career, you must follow up and consistently build on your good initial impressions. When I think about the factors that influenced my success, I realize that the underlying foundation of nearly everything I've accomplished has been what I call "people relations." People relations is the ability to sell yourself to people, to get them to like and respect you. People relations skills—or the lack of them—are on display all the time. They determine the quality of your interactions with your boss, your colleagues, your subordinates, and your friends and acquaintances.

ABOUT PEOPLE RELATIONS

When I first started researching material for *Rogers' Rules for Success,* a book published by St. Martin's Press in 1984, I looked for a theme that had not been covered in the hundreds of success books that have been written over the years. I looked back at my own career and attempted to determine how and why I came to be successful. If I could discover the "secret," that would become the major focus of the book. Was it hard work? I asked myself. Was it drive, energy, dedication, efficiency, persistence? It was all of those, I knew, but there was something else—some hidden key that opened the lock on the box marked SUCCESS.

My mind went back fifty years to the first day I started in the publicity business, in which I eventually put together one of the most prestigious public relations firms in the world. How did it all begin? What steps did I take? What was the breakthrough? If there was a breakthrough, what brought it about? I finally discovered the answer. For the first time, I understood the secret of my success: my ability to relate to people.

I had gone into business for myself with no clients, but with a few influential contacts and a few friends who liked me and who might be willing to open doors for me. They knew that I was struggling to make a living, trying to establish a foothold in the Hollywood community. I assume that they respected me and liked me because they did recommend me to their friends—actors, actresses, motion picture directors, nightclub and restaurant owners—who eventually became my clients. That is how I started in business, and after five or ten years I became reasonably successful.

Once I had established that people relations had been

the key factor in launching my career, I tried to analyze the elements responsible for my *continuing* success. Thinking it through, I concluded that having used my relationships with people to get my career off the ground, I began to study my behavior, modifying it to improve my ability to relate to people.

This self-analysis, which had as its objective a continuing upgrading of my abilities to relate to people, brought me to the point where I am today—not perfect by any means, but certainly far more successful both on the personal and the professional levels than I was fifty years ago.

Based on my experience, I believe you will also find that your ability to learn and practice the art of selling yourself will be the key to a successful career. All you need is a modicum of talent. Couple that with drive, energy, and persistence, and top it all off with knowing and being willing to practice the principles of selling yourself to other people, and you will be well on your way to the top.

TAKING THE FIRST STEPS

The first step in launching your sell-yourself campaign is to evaluate yourself. Who are you? What kind of person are you? What impression do you make on people? Do you turn them on, or do you turn them off? Are you overly emotional? Does it show? Think about your relationships in the business world. Are they good? Bad? Indifferent? Be honest with yourself. Do people seek out your company, or do you feel that they tend to avoid you? Does your boss want to meet with you or does he ignore you? Make a list of your answers to these questions, and any other important factors that you can think of in this self-analysis exercise.

The problem with self-analysis, of course, is that it's almost impossible to be honest with yourself. No one really can. We don't see ourselves as others see us, and inasmuch as the object of this exercise is to improve the perception that your business associates have of you, it is important to find out now what other people think of you.

This is the time to seek out frank, honest counsel and insights from your closest friends and trusted business associates. It may be difficult to get them to open up and tell you the truth—people are reluctant to tell a friend about her faults—but you must insist that you want their honest opinions. Tell them that you are trying to improve yourself, and that you cannot do it without the cooperation of the people who know you best. You're not looking for compliments; you don't want them to tell you how wonderful you are. You want to know what's wrong with you. You want to know which traits in your character turn others off, are misunderstood, and need to be cleaned up or scrapped.

Make two lists: the first is What I Think of Myself; the second one is What Others Think of Me. Study the two lists. Put them together. Think about their similarities and their differences. It is almost obvious what your third list will be: Who I Want To Be. And now that you've identified your goal, it's time to embark on the self-improvement program that will help you to sell yourself to other people.

THE PREREQUISITE: SELF-ESTEEM

The first person you'll have to sell yourself to is yourself. And for many young women (and men, too, incidentally) this is a tough sell. But remember, no one will think much of you if you don't think well of yourself. No one will respect you if you don't respect yourself. And unless you believe in your own ability you can't sell yourself to others.

It's easy for me to tell you this, and it's easy for me to tell you to be secure, but how can you acquire these qualities if you don't already have them? Self-esteem and a sense of personal security in business stem from *knowledge*. If you know as much about your job as anyone in your department, it is only natural that you will enjoy self-esteem. After all, you know as much as the others do, so why rate yourself as worth any less than your colleagues? You may wonder, "But how can I possibly know as much as they do? They've been in their jobs for years, and I've been in mine for only a short time."

Stop and think. You may be better than they are already. It's relatively easy to learn many of the things that more experienced employees know about your jobs. The truth is that there are very few jobs, particularly at an entry level, that cannot be competently learned in a few weeks or months. The reason that it takes most people so long to get up to speed is that they wait to be told by others what to do and how to do it. No wonder it takes them years to learn anything.

You can accelerate the process by teaching yourself. Your self-education program is an intensified version of what you are doing to learn shoptalk. But now you know that there's more at stake than good conversation.

ROGERS' RULES FOR ACQUIRING JOB KNOWLEDGE AND SELF-ESTEEM

1. Read a number of books about your business, or about important people in your business.
2. Read your trade publications regularly.
3. Read the articles in *The Wall Street Journal* about your industry and related industries.

4. Ask questions of the people in your department: How do you do this? Why do we do it this way? What did the boss mean when he said that?
5. Listen carefully when other people talk about business and their jobs.
6. Observe the ways in which other people in your department do what needs to be done. Adapt successful procedures to your own responsibilities.

By reading, listening, and watching, you will, in a few weeks, have a good start on mastering your job. And in a few months, you'll have gained as much knowledge as it might have taken someone else years to acquire. You'll feel better about yourself and your abilities, and you'll actually *be* better. And people will notice that.

Stephanie Barron is the curator of modern and contemporary art at the Los Angeles County Museum of Art. When I asked her whether she considered the term *self-esteem* important to her career success, she responded immediately. "Oh, yes," she said. "When I first arrived at LACMA I was the youngest person who had ever held the lofty position of associate curator. Everyone around me was five to ten years older than I was. I knew that I was capable of performing my job so that I would be respected, so I just said to myself, 'You know your job; forget about your age and get on with it.' I was determined that no one would ever get the opportunity to question my competence, so I overcompensated by putting in a special effort to be as well organized, efficient, and as well directed as I possibly could be. Soon I discovered that my age was a handicap only in *my* mind, and I soon forgot about it."

And in a recent issue of *Savvy*, Patricia Westfall writes,

"On those days when you're feeling outclassed and out-ranked, the key to enhanced self-esteem may lie in taking a close, hard look at those around you." Ms. Westfall describes her early graduate school days when, as a mid-westerner from a lowly state college, she entered an Ivy League institution where, as she recalls, everyone talked "loudly, brilliantly, and constantly." She assumed that they all knew what they were talking about, and was consequently intimidated out of her mind by her new peers—at first.

> I was impressed to the point of terror. I'd sit in seminars with a notepad hidden on my lap, jotting down the name of every unfamiliar book or author the other students mentioned. Stinging from ignorance, I'd race to the library after class and read furiously, trying to catch up with them. After doing this for a few weeks, I realized these name-droppers couldn't possibly have read all the books and writers they were quoting.
>
> Odd scenes followed. Someone would be quoting at length, and I'd gently interrupt, saying, "No, so-and-so didn't write that. What she really said was . . ." There would be a still silence for a moment until the conversation recovered. I think that was when I stopped apologizing.
>
> But what had really happened? I thought I'd just matured. It made sense that if I gained enough knowledge and background to hold my own, then my self-esteem would rise, too.

But, Ms. Westfall recalls, something else had also occurred. "I began to perform well only when I saw my peers as flawed," she writes. "When they seemed like paragons, I was paralyzed. . . . And that leads me to wonder if self-esteem isn't just clear thinking about others."

This is a key point in reinforcing your self-image. Self-esteem is just clear thinking about others. They're not all geniuses. You endow them with brilliance. So you're not limited by your own shortcomings, but by your misperceptions of the "perfection" of others.

BE VISIBLE

Your success is, to a large degree, dependent on other people's recognition of your accomplishments. To sell yourself and your abilities to others, you must be seen. You must be visible.

Maybe your boss knows what you're doing and appreciates your accomplishments, but it's probably better than an even bet that he doesn't. Despite the fact that most bosses try very hard to be tuned in to what their subordinates are doing, they have a difficult time just keeping track of what they themselves are doing. As a result, their subordinates may not get the attention they should receive, and that they need. There is nothing you can do if your boss ignores your associates. But you *can* do something if you sense that he doesn't know what *you're* doing.

ROGERS' RULES FOR MAKING YOURSELF VISIBLE TO YOUR BOSS

1. Make sure your boss knows who you are and what your position is in his department.
2. Ask for a meeting with him at regular periods, and have an agenda of items to discuss that you know will be of interest to him.
3. If he accomplishes something notable and you can sincerely and gracefully praise him, do so.
4. Find opportunities to ask him questions on matters pertaining to your job. It will show him that you are ambitious, and interested in learning as much as you possibly can.
5. Admit it when you are wrong, and recognize that the phrase "I don't know" is a sign of strength, not weakness.

6. Keep him informed of what you are doing. If you send him a memo, make sure it is short and to the point. Bosses hate long memos. (They write them, but they don't read them.)

Once you feel that your boss is becoming aware of your existence, it is now time to turn in other directions. You cannot leave your future entirely in your boss's hands. Where will you be if he moves to another company or another department? He may take you with him, and he may not. You may want to move with him or you may not. Remember that what is in your boss's best interests is not necessarily in *your* best interests. And where will you stand if he gets fired? You will have become recognized as a member of Mr. So-and-so's team, and your career might suffer a setback if he suddenly disappears down a rabbit hole.

The answer to this puzzle, this dichotomy of self-interest, is to make yourself visible and important both to your boss and to other people in the organization. But in doing this, *never* break the chain-of-command commandment. In other words, don't go over your boss's head to solve a problem, present a proposal, etc. Instead, establish strategic relationships outside your department by broadening your acquaintanceships in the company. When you need them, these friends and contacts will be your allies.

VISIBILITY: A CASE STUDY

Debbie Myers, who is associated with the Interdevelopment Bank in Washington, D.C., told me about the steps she took to make herself visible in her organization. "I know that being visible and making my peers and people in top management well aware of my presence is important to my future. I have studied the power structure at the bank, and I know it very, very well. I make it a point, without being pushy or overly aggressive, to establish relationships with members of that power structure."

I interrupted Debbie and asked her how she defined the term *power structure.*

She replied, "I'm referring to the key people who get things done, who execute policy and who make critical decisions. I learned very quickly that the people who comprise the power structure are not necessarily those in top management. They are often people who are moving up rapidly, and who I predict will be the top management of tomorrow.

"I also make a point," she continued, "to have lunch with someone from the bank two or three times a week. I never sit back and wait for an invitation. I invite key colleagues, and in return there are times now and then when they invite me. I also attend each of the occasional bank receptions, and make certain that all the right people are aware of my presence."

If your job and workplace conditions can be compared in any way with Debbie's, I suggest that you use her as one of your role models. I have enormous respect for the manner in which she is conducting her career, and I predict that this young woman, only recently out of graduate school, will one day emerge as one of our most successful businesswomen.

BUILDING YOUR IMAGE IN THE COMPANY

It has often been said that you can't sell a bad product, and the case always used to prove this statement is the Edsel. Many years ago the Ford Motor Company brought

out a new car called the Edsel. It was launched by the
biggest, most expensive advertising, promotion, and public relations program in the history of the automobile industry. Every man, woman, and child in America had
heard about the new Edsel and was anxious to see it. And
when it finally appeared in Ford showrooms, the Edsel was
a disaster. Despite the advertising, the hype, and the public awareness, no one bought it—because it was a bad
product.

I've told you about the Edsel as a prelude to this section
about image, because I want to remind you that my advice
to you in this book hinges on my assumption that you have
some talent, that you work hard, and that you sincerely
want to be successful. Your image in the company is important, but only if you start with these prerequisites.

WHAT IS IMAGE?

You probably hear or read the word every day. Many
U.S. presidents have found their images declining toward
the ends of their terms in office. Ivan Boesky's image was
shattered by his insider trading activities. Libya has a
terrorist image. Senators Bob Dole and Sam Nunn have
favorable images. Joan Collins and Linda Evans have
glamorous images. Beverly Hills has a rich image. Your
professional image, what your boss and your colleagues
think of you, is the most important sales tool you have. It
is one of the key factors that will determine the degree of
success you achieve, and it is a subject worthy of some
thought and effort. You will establish your company image
through your ability to sell yourself to your boss, your
co-workers, your peers, and your subordinates. What do
people really think of you? Do they underestimate you? Or
do they see you as the person you would like to be, hope

to be, and some day will be (if you work hard enough to become that person)?

Many women and men are not aware of the need to create a favorable professional image. The very thought of studying, developing, and maintaining a noteworthy image is completely foreign to them. I don't want it to be foreign to you. From this moment, the word *image* must be on the top of your priority list of words to be thought about and analyzed.

As you become more successful and more visible, your image will be influenced by the evolving concept of femininity. My mother and father would have equated femininity with pink bows and ruffles and lace gloves, with being docile, nurturing, acquiescent, and loving. Germaine Greer, Gloria Steinem, and a number of other leaders have, over the past twenty years, changed our perceptions of femininity, particularly as it pertains to women in the business world.

Women who have had successful careers for ten, fifteen, or twenty years have long ago overcome their fears of trading off femininity and success. They've learned that the qualities that are important in building successful careers, e.g., independence, an interest in achieving power, self-reliance, ambition, and assertiveness, can and do exist together with such traditionally feminine qualities as compassion, empathy, and sensitivity.

SUCCESSFUL WOMEN AND THEIR IMAGES

Barbara Corday, former president of Columbia Pictures Television, told me, "The first time I ever became truly conscious of my image and the impression I was making on my associates was at the time I became an executive at ABC. I was very quiet for the first few months. I felt like a student. I was very self-conscious, unsure of myself, and I decided to sit back and watch. I finally observed that decision making was done by instinct rather than by some magic formula. Once this became apparent to me, I began to assert myself, because I knew that my instincts were as good as anyone else's."

Marketing consultant Dorinda Scharf says, "I have always been aware of my image, conscious of the impression I make on other people. I am sure that my physical appearance helped me to get the jobs I did. There's no doubt that being attractive is helpful, but I always had to prove that I acted older and performed older than I actually was. I have always tried to conduct myself as a serious, no-nonsense woman, but even though I keep trying to improve my image, I'm still not completely happy with myself. I don't deliver as well as I should. My mind works faster than my speech, and I would like to be more effective in this area. I must keep trying to get better."

Stephanie Barron, an associate curator at the L.A. County Museum of Art, told me that she has always been aware of her image, and that she has continued the development of her public image through her work at the museum. "I was always good at lecturing, and I realized very early in my career that this kind of activity could help to develop a public awareness of me in the community. I have always looked for opportunities in museum activities where I could have a public presence. I knew it would help me to achieve the respect I always wanted. However, the public image that I have today is not due solely to my own efforts. Maurice Tuchman, who is my senior curator, helped me to establish my identity and my reputation, because of the opportunities he gave me continually to take on new responsibilities and initiatives. When my colleagues noticed that I was getting respect and support from Maurice, they reacted to me accordingly, and from there on my public image developed in the entire art community."

HAVE SOMETHING IMPORTANT TO SAY

Establishing a favorable image is determined to a great extent by what you say to others. Your conversation must be interesting to the men and women who are your peers and superiors. What do you generally talk about? If you are at all hesitant about your answer, or if your answer does not convince even you that your pet subjects are interesting enough to turn your associates on, then you have another homework assignment ahead of you. If you complete the assignment successfully, you will have important things to say, important subjects to discuss, and important observations to make. How do you do all that? By learning *more* about *more*.

What do your co-workers and your boss talk about during working hours? Management issues? Production problems? Customer relations? New business opportunities? Increased efficiency? How about after work, or at lunchtime? Politics? New films? Real estate?

Whatever they talk about, you should become as knowledgeable about these subjects as anyone in the company. Then you'll feel comfortable participating in conversations with clients and colleagues. You could even sit next to the boss on a four-hour airplane flight and keep him interested—and impressed.

What is the purpose of this study, this self-education,

which will take hundreds of hours of your time every year? The development of a favorable image will advance your career, and it also has a productivity related purpose. While you are developing a favorable image, you are also acquiring knowledge, which, even if it isn't directly related to it, may be helpful in making you better at your job. The knowledge you glean from watching *Today* and *Good Morning America,* or from reading *Time* or *Newsweek,* will make you a more informed person. Being more informed will contribute to your professional skills as a lawyer, an architect, an advertising copywriter, a computer analyst, or any other job to which you are devoting your immediate future.

To get started on this new self-education program, make a list of the topics that are usually discussed in the office, over lunch, at staff or management meetings, or during happy hour when work is over. Watch for articles on these subjects in the magazines and newspapers that you read. Find out which publications and papers your colleagues and your boss read, and add them to your list. Make a point of watching the news and interview shows on TV, and you'll soon find yourself able to contribute to almost any discussion that may arise during the course of doing business. Your image will get a big boost, and you may even discover some subjects that will become lifelong interests.

One last point. Many of the discussions that take place both in and out of the office involve the business you're in. I am a strong advocate of the theory that the quickest and most effective way to become knowledgeable about a particular industry is to read its trade press. Each business has its own set of publications that cover its daily and monthly news developments and trends. If you have not read your particular trade press before, I suggest that you order a few back issues, which will help you to get caught up on recent developments.

DOING HOMEWORK *WORKS*

I recall that many years ago, when I decided to add a contemporary music department to the entertainment division of our public relations firm, I ordered a year's back issues of *Billboard* and *Cashbox*. I plowed through them over weekends for a few months, and by the time I finished I was sufficiently knowledgeable about the contemporary artists of that day, the record labels and the executives who were prominent in each company, the managers, the agents, and the producers to carry on an intelligent conversation about the contemporary music business.

No matter what business you are in, if you are to become a respected participant in discussions with your peers, clients, and other business associates, it is essential that you become a devoted reader of your trade press.

I have often been asked how I keep up with the reading that I need to do to stay abreast of my own business and those of all my clients as well. First, I never do any trade press reading during the course of the working day. Occasionally, if I don't have a lunch date I have a sandwich at my desk, and I can go through a couple of papers in half an hour. Many of my friends do their business reading in the evening, and if that fits your working style I recommend it. I'm not night people, so I prefer to do all my trade paper reading on weekends. Sometime during Saturday or Sunday, I find two or three hours to plow through the stack of publications that has accumulated during the previous week. Remember that you don't have to read every word of every article; skim to find the main issues and the stories most applicable to you and your business.

MANAGING YOUR TIME

When you sit down at your new desk on that first day on the job, the desktop is clean, the drawers are empty. Your first hour or so is taken up with filling out forms and gathering a supply of pens, pencils, paper clips, a stapler, and other supplies. Now take a good look at that clean desktop—this may be the last time you see it.

Within a day or two you will have files and interoffice correspondence piled up in your in-basket; you'll have interim tasks to complete on short-term projects, long-term projects; there'll be staff meetings; you'll have periodic reports to research and write; you'll be interrupted by telephone calls from other departments—how does anyone ever get anything done?

I am able to do everything I want to do without exhausting myself because, over the years, I have developed well-organized work habits. I know what I'm going to do tomorrow, and the next day, and so on throughout the week. In fact, if I show you the pocket calendar that I carry with me every business day, there are dates, events, meetings, conferences, etc. penciled in for the rest of the year, and probably on into next year.

When most people wake up in the morning they have little idea what they will be doing that day. They may know that they have a lunch date at twelve thirty, and a department meeting at four, but other than that, the day's activities usually depend on what happens to be on the person's desk when he or she arrives at the office, or on who is the first to grab his or her attention.

But the most successful women I know are completely in control of their business day, in most cases *before* they leave their offices the night before. Everything is marked down neatly in a notebook or calendar that they carry with them in a briefcase or purse. It's a pleasure to do business with a woman who manages her time this wisely. If I suggest to her that we get together again in thirty to sixty days, she pulls out her calendar, turns to the following month, scans it quickly and says, "Okay, I'll telephone you on October thirtieth and we'll set up a definite appointment." This woman has organized her work habits to achieve maximum efficiency. And intelligent time management is a key ingredient in career success.

The first step toward managing your time wisely is to set up daily, weekly, and monthly *priorities* for the things you have to do. Many people are "too busy" to do everything they need to do because they try to do everything at once. Have you ever spent a really busy day at the office, dashing around from nine in the morning until six in the evening, and as you're ready to leave for home you stop and say, "My God! I didn't get anything done today." It is a frustrating experience that happens all too frequently to many people.

It used to happen to me. At the point in my career that I began to think I had a chance to become successful, I found myself saying "I'm too busy" to nearly everyone, nearly all the time. I was always too busy to do the things I felt had to be done to build a successful business. I was constantly frustrated by the realization that tomorrow had become today, and that what I had planned to accomplish yesterday had not been done at all.

What bothered me most was that I felt I had very well-organized working habits. I loved what I was doing, and the long hours that I put in (usually from seven to seven), didn't bother me. Although I knew that I was gradually moving ahead, there was always the daily frustration of walking into the office every morning and looking at the pile of work on my desk that had been left from the day before. Why couldn't I ever get finished, especially if I was so well-organized?

To me, being well-organized meant taking notes. Early on in my life I realized that I couldn't possibly remember everything, so I developed the habit of carrying a pad and pencil with me at all times. A dozen or twenty or fifty times during the day, whenever I thought of something I needed to do—telephone a client, write a press release, talk to a journalist—I would whip out my pad and pencil and make a note of it. The following morning I would rip all the written pages out of the pad and type up each item on a sheet of paper headed To Do Today. I would also add to the list the items I'd written down the day before that had not been completed.

Being this "well-organized," I couldn't understand why I was too busy to get my work done. Then one day I saw the light. It was seven in the morning. I had just sat down at my desk. The familiar pile of papers lay there with my To Do Today list on top of the stack. As usual, there were many items crossed off: chores that I had finished the day before. But there were still many items remaining. Almost automatically I took my notepad out of my pocket and began to transcribe items that I'd jotted down on the previous day's To Do list. Then I stopped.

I looked at the twelve items that remained from the previous day and realized, for the first time, that these un-crossed-off items were much more important than those I had actually completed. I looked at the sheet of paper again, and once more I studied what I had done the day before, and what I hadn't done. Then came the great awakening: most of what I had done was unimportant; most of what I hadn't done was important.

Although I had always considered myself to be a well-organized person with excellent work habits, at that moment I realized that I had been mistaken. I was always busy—too busy—but I was too busy doing unimportant things. I had no sense of what should have been my *priorities*. Inevitably, as my day began, I would make a comparatively unimportant phone call, dictate an inconsequential memo, or meet with one of my accounts about something that was so insignificant that it really didn't require a meeting.

I had done everything on my list that was easy, that didn't require too much thinking, or any real problem-solving effort. Each of the five or six or ten items that remained unfinished or not even approached required making a special effort. Each was a challenge. I hadn't wanted to face up to the responsibilities of doing the important things because I was afraid I might fail. I just didn't want to face up to the challenge. No wonder I always had the nagging feeling that I wasn't accomplishing anything. I wasn't.

I developed a new procedure that I still use. My To Do list now carries numbers that indicate the importance of each item; it sets priorities for accomplishing each task. Less important items are unnumbered, and all the numbered items are handled first.

ROGERS' RULES FOR SETTING PRIORITIES AND MANAGING YOUR TIME

1. Get into the habit of making lists of things to do every day.
2. Determine as objectively as you can what is truly important, what is less important, and what is unimportant.
3. Discipline yourself to face up to the important mat-

ters and handle them before you even think of starting anything else.

4. Don't tie yourself up with trivia.

5. Never say, "I'm too busy."

6. Once you've gotten used to the habit of organizing
your workdays, organize your weeks, months, etc.

By the way, you can manage your time *out* of the office
the same way: by establishing priorities. Would you join a
health club, read more, take a course, or do volunteer work
if you "only had the time"? Maybe you can get up an hour
earlier, give up a TV show that's more a habit than a
favorite, or skip lunch once a week. If something is really
important to you, you can always find the time to do it.

ASSERTING YOURSELF TO SUCCEED

To be assertive is to express your feelings, needs, and
ideas, and to stand up for your rights in ways that do not
violate the rights of others. Assertiveness is often con-
fused with aggressiveness. But aggressiveness involves
expressing your feelings, needs, and ideas *at the expense
of others;* standing up for your rights *but ignoring the
rights of others.* In being aggressive you dominate, possibly even humiliate other people. That is not your goal.
To be assertive is positive; it is a trait that you should acquire.

Wendy Sukman, a successful stockbroker, talked to me
about the difference between being assertive and being
aggressive. "If a man is aggressive," she said, "he is productive and professional. If a woman is aggressive she is
perceived as being offensive. Right from the beginning of
my career I tried to understand the difference between
being aggressive and being assertive. One person told me

that if I was aggressive I would be coming on to people so that they couldn't respond. When I am assertive, he explained, I give people room for response."

ROGERS' RULES FOR BEING ASSERTIVE

1. Keep increasing your skills. Never stop learning. While you are performing your present job competently, analyze the skills you will require for the job you want to be promoted to, and begin to move in that direction.
2. Learn to say yes at the right times. Look for opportunities to do something for your boss that he or she hasn't asked you to do. Volunteer for assignments that he or she probably would not think of you for, and that spotlight your abilities. Don't ever say, "That's not my job."
3. Ask for what you want. Assume that no one will give you anything voluntarily—a promotion, an increase in salary, a larger office, a plum assignment, a few extra days of vacation, a new desk chair. It's always gratifying if these things come to you over the transom, but understand that if there's something you want, and legitimately deserve, you may have to ask for it.
4. Act confident—even if you don't feel that way. An air of confidence about what you say, what you do, and how you behave, is essential to conveying your ideas assertively.
5. Express your feelings. Wallflowers, the people who hang back, are not the successful ones. Express your feelings at appropriate times, and let people know where you stand.
6. Adopt as role models women you admire who assert themselves. Study the behavior of other women, and adapt to your own style their assertiveness traits.
7. Don't automatically accept unacceptable behavior

from an unfair or even a mean boss. Let him or her know tactfully that you would appreciate being treated with greater consideration.

8. Act—don't react. Don't wait for someone to tell you what to do. Take the initiative, and let people know that you initiate, that you don't wait for things to happen.

A WORD ABOUT OFFICE POLITICS

What is office politics? Why is it so important? Basically, office politics is a way of getting things done. It is a series of strategies used by many different people in an organization, which results in people getting hired and fired, a lower-level manager being moved up to middle management, a vice president appointed senior vice president, and so on. From the mail room to the accounting department, from the assembly line to the executive suites, office politics is an essential part of the process by which companies operate. It is the tool top executives use to compete for power, that secretaries use to win promotions to higher-level jobs, and that managers use to elbow their way through the obstacles to win their cherished vice presidencies.

Office politics is played in every office, in every company, law firm, advertising agency, academic institution, hospital, automotive plant, computer company—anywhere people are working at building their careers. The most energetic participants are those who are eager to move up the corporate ladder. Some people play the game with the highest of ethical principles, and some play cruelly and ruthlessly.

The average newcomer to the business world lacks elementary understanding of the realities of the working environment. That is why the actions and behavior of some of your colleagues may appear so strange to you. But there's no reason why, in today's informed society, you should start a career and not be as prepared to pursue it in all its aspects as anyone else in your company.

There is no rule that states that the practice of office politics is essential. It *is* essential, however, for you to know that it goes on. When you've had a chance to see it in action, then you can decide whether you want to become a player. Much of your decision will depend on how ardently and how fiercely you want to pursue a career in today's corporate world. It is possible to be successful in other ways, avoiding the chutes and ladders of corporate politics.

To understand the term *office politics,* you first need to accept that in the long run your success is not determined solely by how well you complete the tasks you've been assigned: it is just as important to be *perceived* as competent as it is to perform competently. Furthermore, organizations are made up of people, not machines. Some people get along, some don't. Some will do anything to increase their power and salaries. Some criticize their colleagues behind their backs. Some will do anything to hold on to their jobs, even if others in the organization may suffer as a result. You'll find colleagues who are self-assured, and insecure ones too. Some people are considered easy to work with and others aren't. As it turns out, whenever people have to apply their judgment to a subjective decision, simple human emotion is bound to play a role, and that's where office politics comes into play.

You know about political campaigns—the intrigue, the maneuvering for advantage, the importance of public opinion, the lust for power, the doing of favors in exchange for favors done. You're aware that some members of the U.S.

Congress are considered more powerful than others, that in some cases people are powerful if they're *perceived* as such and, alternately, may lack influence even if their titles and seniority are impressive. All of these truths apply to daily life in a corporation as well. You will see one vice president become a senior vice president in record time, while another worker is fired on that same day. One person is moved to a corner office, while another moves from an office into the bullpen.

The object of the game—let's be frank about this—is acquiring money and power. If you want money and power, you must learn to play. If you really don't care that much about either, there is no need for you to be a participant; you can live a happy, fulfilled life without doing so.

YOU DON'T HAVE TO PLAY

My impression is that if you wish to make it big in the corporate world, playing office politics is close to essential. If it is a subject, however, that offends you, or if you decide that you just don't want to be a player, you can switch careers or go off in a different direction that doesn't call for you to struggle in the corporate hierarchy. Let's hear from two friends of mine who decided not to play the game.

Betty Goodwin is a successful freelance writer in Los Angeles. She worked in important positions in that city's two metropolitan newspapers but gave up working in both organizations after deciding that working in a corporate organization did not fit her style or her needs. She says, "In regard to office politics, I am not very good at it. I was never able to make friends with my superiors. I guess I never tried. Some people do it well. I never could or never wanted to. Some people are masters at this. Some people are able to associate with the top people in the organization, and they've developed skills along that line. I marvel at their ability to do that. Maybe that's why I dropped out. Freelancing is free of political games and office politics."

Dorinda Scharf, president of Logistix International, a small marketing consulting firm in the fragrances and cosmetics business, agrees. "I'm sure that some women are good at it. I'm not, and I hate it. I had a very important job with Estée Lauder, but I left after two years because I just couldn't, or didn't want to, play the political game any longer.

"I never knew who my boss was. I had to deal with enormous egos, and I spent sixty percent of my time politicking. It was too tough, and when I received an offer to go with the newly established Warner Cosmetics, which was just about to launch a line of Polo fragrances by Ralph Lauren, I jumped at the chance.

"Well, we all keep learning, and I soon discovered that money and perks don't necessarily mean job satisfaction. I found myself working for dictatorial, authoritarian bosses, who squeezed us and pressured us mercilessly. I was surrounded by megalomaniacs in a bureaucratic atmosphere I didn't like. I knew it was time to make another change. I wanted to have fun at my job, and I wasn't having any, so I decided to interview with a number of companies. I did, and soon realized that bureaucracy and office politics exist in most companies, that that was not the kind of business life I wanted to lead, and that I had to look for an opportunity to go into business for myself. It was time for me to determine my own destiny and establish for myself a work environment that was right for me. It was then that I established my own consulting business, and I've never regretted it."

I am not critical of my young friends who don't want to participate in office politics. It requires enormous effort, and it can be nerve-wracking, as has been pointed out by Betty and Dorinda. Before you opt out, however, you should know what office politics is all about. Study your present work environment. You will soon begin to distinguish between the people who are really focused on success, and those who aren't.

IF YOU DECIDE TO PLAY, PLAY TO WIN

If you throw your hat into the political ring, you'll find a role model or two very helpful. Focus on those people whose ways of dealing with people you admire, whose behavior you respect, and who are successful or appear to be on the road to success. Once you've assimilated some basic skills by observing your role models, you're ready to enter the arena and begin to play the game.

Office politics is played on many levels. You must decide at what level you want to play, and by what rules. Through your period of observing your colleagues you will have gotten some insights into which rules appear to achieve the best results. But feel free to take the best of other people's rules of thumb and adapt them to your style.

Anne Luther, director of public relations for Schieffelin & Company, importers of fine wines and spirits, says, "Don't think of politics as a dirty word. Doing your job is not enough if you wish to be successful. It is important to establish friendships within your organization. And keep current with what is going on. By keeping yourself tuned in, you can stay abreast of what management considers to be the top priorities at any particular moment."

Phyllis Kaminsky, director of United Nations Information Center in Washington, learned to play the game many years ago and has been playing it successfully ever since. The key to her success in office politics is summed up in a few observations Phyllis made to me the other day. "I am a political animal," she said, "and I play the game according to what I believe are the Washington rules. When I receive a telephone call from someone, I always take it, even though I may not be familiar with the name, because I feel there may be a payoff later on."

Stephanie French, a public affairs executive with the Philip Morris Company, has this to say about office politics. "I hate it, but I guess it's something that has to be dealt with in a big company like ours. I resent the time I spend demonstrating how good our department is, and the necessity for covering your ass all the time. I wish I could just do my job and not have to concern myself with countering the activities of people who encroach on my area."

I talked to many different women while I was researching this book. Here is a sampler of their views on office politics.

- "I developed a procedure a long time ago that has worked very efficiently for me. I do something for someone, or at least express my willingness to do something for them, before I ask for anything. I find that people more readily respond to my requests if I have first made an offer of help."
- "I try to be nice to everyone. It's not so much a matter of the old adage, 'Be nice to people when you're on the way up because you might meet them on the way down.' It's just that I have found that a smile or a kind word comes back to me tenfold. If I'm kind to people, they're kind to me."
- "I never discuss my personal affairs in the office. I don't believe that anyone should know that I went to the den-

tist, or took a new lover, or bought a new dress. In the office I talk business only, and keep my personal life completely apart from my business life."
- "I've learned to listen, and I find that it's tremendously advantageous in my job. Most people don't listen. They're too busy talking, and as a result, they really don't know what's going on in the office. By listening I keep myself very well informed."
- "It took me a long time to stop saying, 'Don't tell anybody, but . . .' I learned that if there's something I don't want others to know about, I'm better off not talking about it. There is no such thing as a confidential communication. It always gets repeated."

Finally, here are my thoughts on playing the game of office politics.

ROGERS' RULES FOR PLAYING OFFICE POLITICS LIKE A PRO

1. Let people know that you're interested in getting ahead, but don't let them know that you hope to be president of the company someday.
2. Don't be in awe of people in high places.
3. Getting along is the essence of getting ahead, so it is essential to establish amicable relationships with bosses, peers, and subordinates.
4. Emulate people you respect and admire. Adopt their best characteristics and make them part of your own style.
5. There are no fixed rules for playing politics. You can develop your own, provided that they conform to the generally accepted code of play in your company.
6. You can win the game of office politics by being personable, honest, and ethical. Don't believe baseball's

famous Leo Durocher's oft-quoted observation, "Nice guys finish last." Nice people *do* have successful careers.

7. Making your boss feel important is a pathway to your success. If ego-stroking is not your style, give serious consideration to changing your style.

8. Lose the battle and win the war. I've said this hundreds of times, but I must repeat it once more because it is essential in office politics. Don't sacrifice long-term career advancement by scoring a relatively unimportant victory today.

5

Career-Building Strategies

Now that you've landed a career-path job, what next? This chapter will present a number of career-building strategies that will help to maximize your chances of success. Your questions about interviews and finding out about job opportunities will now be replaced by a new set of questions. Should you take risks or should you play it safe? How will you deal with an unanticipated offer of a promotion or a new job outside your company? If you've made a mistake in your job choice, how can you cut your losses with the least amount of pain and the least damage to your career? To whom should you turn for career advice now?

These and a thousand other questions are probably in your mind, and if they aren't, they should be. You won't become successful just by chance, or by good luck. Sure, you might get a lucky break and land a cushy job without much effort. But how long will you keep it, and what should you do to eventually move from that job to an even better one?

To get your career moving in the right direction, and to keep it on course in the years to come, there are certain work-smarter guidelines that you should become familiar with. In the following pages you will find some of these rules of thumb, which I advise you to keep in mind for both present and future reference.

FIND A MENTOR

The whole subject of mentoring may be unclear to you, so let me define it. A mentor is someone who sees possibilities in a younger person and helps to bring that person along. There are enormous advantages to having a mentor. As I stated earlier, most women find themselves in a foreign environment when they enter the workplace, and having a coach standing by ready to help you find your way, to translate business jargon into language that you can understand, and to guide you in your relationships with your colleagues and your boss gives you a leg up on your peers who don't enjoy the advantages of a counselor. And mentors are not just for rookies. Many successful women turn to mentors for guidance during the entire course of their careers.

Mentors can be of either sex, but they must of necessity be higher up the ladder than you are, and older as well. A mentor is someone who can give perspective to your situation by letting you know how others see you, someone who will speak well of you in high places. He or she can give you valuable political advice, telling you who is dangerous, who can help you, and who can damage your chances for advancement. Your mentor can help you decide which projects you should get involved with and give you advance warning of impending disasters, providing the guidance you need to successfully handle those situations. He or she sees you as a protégée whose success will reflect on his or her astuteness in selecting you for tutorship. But your mentor will continue to give you time, attention, and "inside information" only if you prove worthy of his or her support.

A ROLE MODEL IS NOT A MENTOR

Don't confuse mentors with role models and sponsors. A role model for you is a woman who has achieved a high position in the business world, thus proving to you that it can be done. She may not even be aware of your existence, and that is not important. All that matters is that she exists for you to emulate. A sponsor is someone you can occasionally seek out for advice, someone who holds a job higher than yours, who is aware of you and your talents and who will recommend you for assignments and promotions, even though he or she may not take the time to coach you in the ways of the corporate world.

YOU MUST LOOK FOR A MENTOR—OR THREE

It is highly unlikely that a male or female executive will walk into your office one day and say, "Here I am; I'm your mentor." It just doesn't happen that way. You will find a mentor by getting to know people up, down, and across the organization. If you find that there's an older colleague to whom you naturally go when you need advice about a specific task, someone who also sometimes volunteers additional advice about the company, that person might be a potential mentor. In fact, your mentor may not even work at your company. Your business network may be a good place to start seeking out potential mentors. The perfect situation is to find several mentors, at least one of whom is a woman. You should look for people who are somewhat older than you, who are among the recognized power group in the organization, and who are willing and able to coach and train you.

Jane Frank Harman, a lawyer associated with the Jones & Day office in Washington, D.C., had the good fortune to receive helpful mentoring from Senator John Tunney and other bosses over the years. "I was always fortunate to have the support of the men who helped me to learn what I had to learn to do my job effectively," she told me recently. "Senator John Tunney helped me enormously. I went to work for him in 1972 as his legislative assistant for environmental affairs. I was decidedly unqualified to take on such an important assignment at that point in my career, but I learned on the job with the senator's help and guidance."

Lisa Specht, a successful Los Angeles attorney, says, "One of the most important things you can do is look for a mentor. I was fortunate to find one in Alan Rothenberg, one of the senior members of our firm. He helped me enormously. I never asked him to be my mentor. Instead, I kept asking him for assignments, asking him for advice, and he became my mentor without even realizing it. If you can set your sights on someone in a position of power, someone you respect, and subtly inject yourself into his life so that he becomes your mentor, you will find that it will give your career a decided lift and put you on the path to success."

Jan West has had a variety of jobs since she finished her

graduate studies. She is currently an entrepreneur, partnered with a male friend as media broadcast consultants. Her advice: "Keep in contact with people who have interviewed you for jobs, and any other people you meet in business who have higher positions than you have, and eventually you will find someone who will volunteer to be your mentor." To expand on Ms. West's advice about keeping in contact, my recommendation is that after sending the person who has just interviewed you a thank-you note, some weeks later send him a magazine or newspaper clipping that might interest him, and every few months send a note reminding him of your continued interest. Be sure to approach and reintroduce yourself if you spot him at an trade or industry association meeting, or even at a restaurant. Never be shy about approaching people you may have met only once or twice.

THE MALE MENTOR

One of the pitfalls of having a male mentor is that your collaboration may be seen as—and may actually develop into—a sexual relationship. This may not be harmful to your career, but the odds are great that in the long run the resultant office gossip can hurt you personally and professionally. Both female and male executives agree that this situation should be avoided, but these executives also realize that when people are attracted to each other the temptations which lead to a sexual relationship can be great. Some good advice:

• Treat your mentor like your father or a helpful uncle.
• Don't get into discussions about your personal life.
• Avoid meeting alone with him after normal business hours. This kind of activity just stirs up gossip.

• If you fear that the two of you are becoming the target of office gossip, don't be reluctant to discuss it with Mr. Mentor. If his intentions are honorable, he'll adjust his behavior.

One way to defuse the sexual slant of a male mentoring situation is to acquire several mentors. A young woman executive friend of mine told me, "Men in my company just didn't run the risk of acting as a mentor to a woman because of the inevitable gossip that would result. So what I did was prove my abilities to several men, in the hope that more than one would sponsor me for a promotion or choose me to work on a special project. When more than one man seemed to be championing me, it took the pressure off any individual. Eventually, I gained several mentors this way, and now I always try to have at least three. Any sexual implications have become so diffused that it no longer interests the gossips. I have also found another way that this safety in numbers works for me. When one of my mentors fell from grace, I didn't go down with him. I had other people to depend upon, and was not too closely attached to any one person."

THE FEMALE MENTOR

The sexual implications of mentorship are virtually eliminated, of course, if you win a woman executive over to your cause. However, many successful women are reluctant to commit to mentoring young women because they are so busy fighting to keep what they've got and promote their own futures. And you may be a woman who finds it difficult to accept a woman as a mentor. If you feel this way, you're not alone. Many of your peers have similar feelings. Psychologists explain that the reason for this resistance is that women have been socialized to see each other as rivals. Consultant Arleen La Bella says, "Since we were young, most women have been raised to think that the best we could do is to land a successful man, and that we are in competition with all other women to find that man. From the early years on, other women are not our collaborators but our competitors."

Fortunately, this attitude is changing, and it should not deter you from seeking or accepting help from a female mentor.

ROGERS' RULES FOR FINDING A MENTOR

1. Understand how he, she, or they can help your career.
2. Try to get two or three mentors. Divergent points of view are healthy; they prevent tunnel vision.
3. Seek advice from your mentor, taking as much of his time as he can afford to give you.
4. Don't hesitate to mention work-related problems, insecurities, and fears. Your mentors won't know how to help you unless they know the areas in which you need help and guidance.
5. Be flexible about your mentors' time constraints. Time spent together must be at their convenience, not yours.
6. Be assertive and self-confident in your dealings with your mentors. You must be perceived as a success-oriented person.
7. Don't get discouraged if you don't find a mentor right away. Good ones are hard to find. Until you do, line up what I call a sponsor or two—a person you can occasionally seek out for advice. When you finally find your mentor, he or she will be willing to spend more time with you.

THE CONTINUING IMPORTANCE OF NETWORKING

As I've already mentioned, networking is a skill that you should become adept at, and that you should continue throughout your working life. Why is it so important?

Dr. Samuel Johnson probably said it first: "The next best thing to knowing something is knowing where to find it." That just about sums up why networking can be of enormous help to you in your career. Your networking contacts can answer your questions about almost anything—your job, the company you work for, the industry or particular business that interests you, and so on. And most important, your contacts can tell you where the best—and worst—career opportunities are.

There is currently a profusion of professional networking organizations scattered throughout the United States, in which women and men in all occupations trade business cards, information, advice, and referrals. I urge you to get in touch with any networking groups that are available to you. You can probably trace down two books in your local library that will give you valuable information and will identify the networking organizations that have branches in the city where you live. These books are *Networking: The First Report and Directory* by Jessica Lipnack and Jeffrey Stamps, and *Women's Networks* by Carol Kleiman. I also suggest that you seek information from the International Alliance, an association of women's organizations that serves as a central forum for twenty-five professional women's networks in the United States. And get in touch with the National Women's Forum, which has chapters in fifteen American cities. From these sources, you should be able to ascertain which organizations most interest you. They can be invaluable to your future career advancement.

I recently had an experience that demonstrates the continuing importance of networking. I was having lunch in New York one day with Joan Wechsler, a longtime friend who had recently left an executive position at the ABC television network. Even though I knew she was overqualified for the position, I offered her the job of managing my New York office. As I expected, she turned me down, but said, "I know a young woman at ABC who is very unhappy in her job. She would be perfect for you." The next day Vicki Vasquez telephoned. She came up to the office, I spoke with her for a few minutes, and, impressed with her obvious qualifications, I passed her on to two other people in our office who would make the final decision. Two weeks later Vicki Vasquez stepped into the position of New York office manager for Rogers & Cowan, and she's doing an excellent job.

ALWAYS BE ALERT TO OPPORTUNITY

One characteristic that separates the successful woman from the rest of the herd is her ability to perceive opportunities where other people see only problems, complications, or nothing at all. Being alert to opportunities, and being able to take advantage of them when they arise, can help you to leapfrog over the competition as they proceed in orderly fashion from point A to point B, never realizing that there is any other way to go.

You never know when or where opportunity may present itself, so you should have your antennas up all the time—at the office, at social events, even at home as you catch up on your reading. Be ready to open the door when opportunity knocks. If a new job unexpectedly opens up in your company, be the first one to ask for it. If you are given the opportunity to meet someone who could be important to your career, don't pass it by because you had planned to clean out your closet that night.

Let's say that one day you are invited to a business-related cocktail party. You're tired, you've had a rough day; you really don't feel like going, and no particular deal is riding on your presence there, so you really don't *have* to go. But one of your colleagues talks you into going anyway. You walk into the party and start to mingle. You meet a number of people, one of whom is the executive vice president of one of your company's major competitor. When he discovers what you do, he asks you to have lunch with him the following week. You accept. During lunch, after talking with you for an hour, he offers you a great job—more money, more responsibility, the title you've been working for. If you had passed up the opportunity to broaden your network of contacts, you wouldn't have been presented with this terrific opportunity.

Here's a real-life example of a woman who was smart enough to answer the door when opportunity knocked. Kathie Berlin headed up the entertainment division of our New York office for more than ten years. During most of that time, Marlo Thomas was a Rogers & Cowan client. Marlo has been very successful as an actress, and as a producer of television specials and made-for-TV movies. Our office handled the publicity for those projects, and because Marlo is in New York rather than in Hollywood, the responsibility for getting the job done was Kathie Berlin's.

Marlo and Kathie became very close over the years. Marlo developed a great respect for Kathie over and above her ability in the public realtions area. She respected her as a woman, for her intellectual abilities, and for her business and creative judgment. Carole Hart, another television client, also became a friend of Kathie's. When the time came for Marlo and Carole to set up their own independent television production company, they asked Kathie to come in with them as an equal partner. Naturally, Kathie accepted. It was a fabulous opportunity, and it was the right time for her to make a career change. I was sad for us, but very happy for her.

Sometimes just flipping through a magazine presents an opportunity, if your mind is open to new ideas at all times. Paula Meehan, president of Redken Laboratories, told me, "I had been in the hair-care products business for several years when I happened to read an article in a magazine about Vidal Sassoon, who at that time was the most important hairdresser in London. I decided that it would be a good idea to bring him to the United States to serve as a spokesman for Redken hair products. I made a financial arrangement with him, and the timing was right because we had just introduced the Redken permanent wave. I took him on a tour of the United States, and it was all enormously successful. It gave our company a big shot in the arm." Vidal Sassoon went on to become an important figure in the hair-care products business on his own, but at that moment in time, Paula's business got a tremendous boost because she was creative enough to see the connection between an article about a high-profile hairdresser and her business.

Life tosses fly balls like these at everybody, but only the achievers know how to catch them. Wendy Sukman is a broker at Paine Webber in Beverly Hills. She sat in my office one day and told me, "The phone was ringing one day and no one was answering it. I picked up the phone and chatted for a few minutes with the man who was calling. He wasn't calling anyone in particular, he just wanted to place an order to buy a hundred shares of stock at twelve dollars a share. I handled it for him, and as a result of cultivating him on the phone on a continuing basis he is now one of my biggest accounts."

BROADEN YOUR HORIZONS

I can think of nothing more important in enhancing your career—and your life—than to broaden your horizons. If you have accepted my premise that one of the basic keys to success is your ability to relate to people and to impress them, then it is essential that you become knowledgeable on a wide range of subjects. Most people are not able to discuss anything other than their own personal interests, and those interests are usually severely limited. This is unfortunate for all your competitors, but fortunate for you. If you are able to broaden your horizons and to understand and discuss topics outside your own immediate interests, you will be regarded as a special person. And I'll remind you that it is the special person, not the ordinary person, who succeeds.

Let's return to my recurring theme of relating to and impressing people, and let's concentrate for the moment on your boss. We have already established that it is to your advantage to be visible to him, to relate well to him, and to consistently impress him. If he is a Boston Celtics fan, will he be impressed if you are able to chat with him about how many points Larry Bird racked up against the Lakers last night? If he is interested in contemporary art, will he be impressed if he unexpectedly meets you at an opening at a local gallery or museum one evening? If you know that he watches *The MacNeil/Lehrer News Hour,* will he

be impressed if you ask him for his opinions on what senators Dole and Packwood discussed about the tax reform
bill Monday night? The answer to each question, of course,
is *yes*. Your boss will definitely be impressed with your
interests in so many different subjects.

I am reminded of where and how I met Debbie Myers,
the young career woman from Washington whom I've
mentioned several times in this book. She was my class-
mate at Cambridge University in England for three weeks
during the summer of 1986. What was I doing there?

Five years before, my wife and I had discovered that the
University of California at Berkeley had an extension summer study program at Oxford. We became intrigued with
the idea of going back to school, and the opportunity of
going to Oxford University in England made it particularly appealing to us. We looked over the curriculum and
decided that Twentieth-Century British Drama was the
course we'd most like to take. That three-week course was
the most enjoyable and satisfying vacation we ever had.
Soon after, when we learned that UCLA had a similar
summer program at Cambridge University, we agreed to
repeat our adult educational experience at the earliest possible time. That turned out to be 1986. I selected a course
in British economics and politics.

We were a class of fourteen, of whom Debbie was one.
At this writing, I don't know whether Debbie's career has
advanced since we first met, but I am willing to wager that
she is in a better position today, makes more money, and
has a more prestigious job than when she departed from
Washington one hot day in July, 1986, bound for Cambridge University to broaden her horizons.

I never asked her whether she had enrolled in that
summer study program for career reasons. I have a
hunch that she never thought of it in those terms. If

she'd planned to go to school to enhance her career, she would most likely have looked for a course in international banking or inter-American finance, subjects directly related to her job at that time. But I believe that Debbie took the course in British economics and politics simply to increase her knowledge of a subject that interests her. I'm certain that she never thought about how much she would impress people as a result of her three-week experience at Cambridge.

One can imagine what might have happened to Debbie after she returned to her job in Washington. At a dinner party one night, a guest commented on the unemployment problem in Great Britain. Debbie, in an unassuming manner, entered the conversation. "When I studied that subject at Cambridge University this past summer, I learned that . . ." The other guests were stunned to find out that this young woman had actually spent her holiday going to school instead of sunning herself on a beach, and that she was very knowledgeable on the subject of unemployment in the U.K. She could speak equally knowledgeably on the Falklands war, the turmoil in Northern Ireland, monetarism as an economic policy, socialized medicine, and a dozen other fascinating subjects that we covered during our course.

You might ask, "Didn't Debbie become a bore with all this highbrow talk? Didn't people just feel that she was boasting and showing off?" Good questions, I grant you, and I must offer another imaginary scenario to answer them. Debbie is an unusually bright, ambitious career woman. She is very sensitive to the impression she makes on people, and I am confident that she used her knowledge wisely. She knew when to pick up the thread of a conversation, and when to back away. I am confident that Debbie used her newly broadened horizons to enhance her career and to subtly impress the people she felt were important to impress.

THE KEY: LEARN MORE ABOUT MORE

What does it mean, to broaden your horizons? Simply, learn *more* about *more*, and become interested in more than just your job or your social life. Learn about what? you may ask. How about these topics: art, music (pop and classical), world affairs, sports, science, astronomy, astrology, history, advertising, medicine, computer science, theater, movies, archaeology, the Far East, the Third World, Soviet-American relations, politics, problems of the inner city, education. These are just a few subjects with which you can begin to broaden your horizons. But if you are like some young women I know, you might say to me, "But I'm not interested in any of those subjects."

This brings me to a memorable book I read many years ago. It is titled *I Like What I Know,* and it was written by Vincent Price, a gentleman you see frequently on television, either in commercials or as the star of vintage horror movies. Mr. Price, an art collector, connoisseur, and critic as well as a successful actor, wrote this book as an answer to the uninformed, narrow-minded people who reject learning anything new about art by saying, "I don't know anything about art, but I know what I like." Mr. Price argues that this is not really the case. These people don't know what they like, *they like what they know.* They like scenic postcards and calendar art because that may be the only "art" they've ever looked at. How do you know what you like, he asks, if you don't broaden your horizons beyond your childhood experiences?

My advice to you is to try everything, experience everything, take a stab at everything, until you find one or more areas of interest that really turn you on. The whole world is out there waiting for you to pick it up, savor it, taste it. You'll find that broadening your horizons isn't work. It's fun.

PLAYING THE POWER GAME

You hear the word *power* every day at your office. People say, "That guy has power," or, "He's just lost his power base," or, "She's trying to become a power around here." As a society, we have an ongoing love affair with power; we have power breakfasts, power brokers, powers of attorney, superpowers, and powers of persuasion. What is power all about? Is it important to you? Is it worth the effort it takes to get it? These are all logical questions, and I'll do my best to answer them for you.

Power, in the context of your career, is the ability to persuade and influence people. Power is knowing what you want and how to get it.

- W. Antoinette Ford, assistant administrator of the Agency for International Development, says, "Power is having the charisma, control, and confidence to cause others to believe that you have something they need or want."
- Political scientists Harold Laswell states, "Power is simply who gets what, when, where, and how."
- Laurel Cutter, one of advertising's most powerful women, sums it all up when she says, "Power is when you talk, people listen."

Any woman who seeks success in business knows that she must work, fight, and struggle to move from a subordinate to a superior position. She knows how to work and she works hard, knowing that this is the price of getting what she wants. She knows that her purpose is not just to make money, but also to be rewarded in terms of gratification, autonomy, and independence.

Within your organization, each job carries with it a certain degree of power. Whether you're an assistant account executive in an advertising agency or the president of the company, a measure of power comes with the territory. But the power inherent in the job is meaningless if you don't know what to do with it. The extent of the power you exert will be determined by your ability to improve and perfect the talents and skills that won you your job in the first place.

First, you must become proficient at your job and know as much about it as anyone else in the company. You can't get others to do what you want them to do unless they respect your abilities and accomplishments.

Once you've become an ace at your job, you must make sure that you are relating well to the people you work with, and that you've developed an ability to assess the unspoken reactions of your colleagues. If you can tune into this kind of feedback about how your ideas and behavior are being perceived, you will be in a position to maximize your ability to influence others.

It is important for you to learn to influence people without making them subservient. We are working in a business environment in which people are more independent than they have ever been before. Back at the turn of the century, employers could treat their employees as servants and get away with it. Today, the talented people whom you want to work with you expect to be treated with courtesy and respect. And if they don't get it, they will go elsewhere for it.

Learning to use power effectively is one of the most

difficult tasks you'll face as you become more successful. Just remember: the greater the potential power, the greater the responsibility.

ROGERS' RULES FOR PLAYING THE POWER GAME

1. Ask for the toughest and most important assignments.
2. Help your boss to do his job better. As he goes up the corporate ladder, you'll go with him.
3. Know where the power in your organization is, and get close to it. Get to know and try to establish a relationship with the decision makers. You may be able to influence their decisions as they pertain to you.
4. Once again, make yourself visible to top management.
5. Praise your boss, both directly and to others. It will make you look even better.
6. Make a point of being liked and respected.
7. Make decisions and take risks. Don't be afraid to make mistakes.
8. Be flexible: take a little and give a little.

KEEPING YOUR EYE ON A GOAL

It is always important to have one or more career goals in sight. These goals will inevitably change as you progress through your career, but they give your efforts a necessary focus. Susan Horowitz is presently director of current programming at Warner Brothers Television. I sat next to her on a flight from New York to Los Angeles one day and struck up a conversation. I began to ask her about her career and the goals she has had. She said, "I went to Queens College in New York. At that time I was only interested in the art world. I wanted to be a sculptor, and I worked hard at it, but then I became aware that I was not good enough to be successful in that field. The idea of being successful was already important to me, and I realized that in order to achieve my goal I had to give up my hopes for an art career.

"I took a job as a secretary, which proved to be a door-opener for me. Just at that time I met the man who is now my husband. He is Rick Feldman, vice president and station manager of KCOP-TV in Los Angeles. He introduced me to a woman at the Diener-Hauser advertising agency. She, in turn, introduced me to Donald Rugoff, a New York theater operator who was looking for an advertising director. I had no background for the position, but I was able to talk him into giving me the job, because he was an art collector and I talked to him about art.

A STEPPING-STONE TO SUCCESS

"He paid me seventeen thousand dollars a year, which was twice as much money as I had ever been paid before. This was the stepping-stone I had been looking for, and I worked hard at my job. Even though I didn't particularly like advertising, I felt that it could lead me to the film business, which had by then become my goal. In addition to designing ads, I went to screenings and learned a lot about the movie industry. I was with Rugoff for a year until one day he fired me. This was a traumatic experience, but it shouldn't have been. It was generally known in the industry that if you were fired by Don Rugoff you were a talented, normal human being. That was his reputation.

"While I was living on unemployment, I kept on reading the key trade publications and networking whenever I could to extend my contacts in advertising and in film. I

read one day that Twentieth Century Fox had just left the
Diener-Hauser agency and had moved its account over to
Doyle Dane Bernbach. Doyle Dane refused to interview
me for the job of account executive, for which I felt qualified because of my Rugoff experience. Claude Lewis, head
of advertising for Twentieth Century, was one of the contacts I had made over the course of my career. He liked me
and respected my ability, and he agreed that I was qualified for the job. He used his prerogative as the client to
recommend to DDB that they hire me. They had no choice.
They did it.

"I was the account executive on the Twentieth Century
Fox account at DDB for three years," Susan continued as
we flew 36,000 feet above the earth. "I knew that I was
good enough to be a vice president, and although there
were no women VPs at Doyle Dane at the time, I worked
to get the title. I was relentless, and I asked for it repeatedly. Finally, after five years, they promoted me. I was a
vice president of Doyle Dane Bernbach.

"DDB was an important career move for me, and I
stayed there for nine and a half years when Rick, with
whom I was living at the time, moved to Los Angeles in his
present position at KCOP-TV. I rearranged my job so that
I could spend time there, too, and I became a bicoastal
woman, commuting regularly between New York and L.A.
Once I started to make trips to the West Coast I began to
look for a new job, knowing that that was where Rick
would be headquartered from now on.

"I was offered two jobs, and I accepted the offer of
director of current programming at Warner Brothers Television. I took a cut in salary, which I was willing to do
because I felt that the job was a step up. I knew that it was
a job where I could meet everyone in the entertainment
business very quickly. We have eight shows on the air, I

am broadening my experience every day, and I know that I'm on my way to a very successful career in Hollywood."

THE RIGHT MOVES

Susan made a number of important moves during the course of her career, which deserve to be looked at more closely. She didn't get to her present prestigious position just by luck. Success came because she had both the courage and the drive to make decisions, rather than sitting back and letting nature take its course, as so many of us have a tendency to do.

Susan's first important career move came when she admitted to herself that she was not sufficiently talented as a sculptor to make art her life's work. Accepting our limitations is something that we should have the courage to do, no matter how painful it might be.

Next, she quickly discovered the advantages of networking, getting out to meet people who could help her. Her first breakthrough with Donald Rugoff and her second job at Doyle Dane Bernbach both came through recommendations from people she had met and cultivated.

Finally, when the man who was to become her husband moved to Los Angeles, she convinced her boss that it was to his advantage for her to become bicoastal. Once she set this up she was able to see the man she loved regularly. She simultaneously set her sights on a permanent Hollywood position, which she accepted at a substantial salary cut because she knew it would open the door to the movie career that was her long-term goal.

There is a big difference between acting and reacting. Susan is a perfect example of a woman who makes things happen rather than waiting for things to happen to her.

TAKING RISKS

Taking risks covers a broad spectrum of behavior, some of which might be appropriate to those new to the work world, and some of which is more appropriate for career women who've had a few or many years of experience. For an editorial assistant at a magazine, taking a risk might be sending the editor a memo about a new story idea; in an advertising agency, a junior media planner recommending the addition of a cost-effective but hitherto untested magazine to a media schedule might be an example of the right kind of risk.

As an employer, I respect my female associates who take the responsibility for their own decisions. Making decisions inherently involves taking risks. And you will never be a leader, you will never head your department, you will never move up the corporate ladder unless you are willing to take risks. You must have the courage to take positive actions and make important decisions, decisions that could prove to be incorrect. What will your boss say if you're wrong? If he or she is a smart and experienced manager, you will probably be told that it is better to do *something*, even if it is later proven a mistake, than to play it safe and do nothing. To use a baseball metaphor, you won't become a successful hitter if you stand at the plate and never swing at the ball. If you keep swinging, you may occasionally strike out, but you will also get your share of home runs.

It is important for you to realize that you can be a decision maker and still seek out help when you need it (and if you're smart, you'll know that you need it all the time). Keep asking questions; every time you get an answer, you'll be learning just a little bit more about your job, and about the situation that requires your decision. Don't be reluctant to say to one of your fellow workers, "I think I'm on the right track here, but I would like to have your opinion." You will be respected for this approach. In fact, the person from whom you ask advice will be flattered that you have singled him or her out for guidance.

I have never figured out why people are so reluctant to ask questions or seek advice. I've been doing it all my life. I recall one day many years ago when a friend of mine said, "You're a brain-picker." I regarded it as a compliment. No one is expected to know everything about everything.

The risks of day to day decision making can be seen to pale by comparison with the risks involved in major career decisions. In keeping your career plan flexible enough to respond to new opportunities, you may be faced with a choice between the comfort of security or the exhilaration of a chance to enter a new and unknown world. To leap or not to leap? It may be helpful for you to hear how a number of successful women have taken risks during the course of their careers and have been rewarded for their courage and their belief in themselves.

Tina Brown emerged on the New York publishing scene a few years ago as editor of the once failing, now successful magazine *Vanity Fair*. She has quickly become one of the most discussed, most popular women in her field. We sat at lunch one snowy winter day at the Algonquin Hotel in New York. She looked around the room and commented, "I always come here for lunch for nostalgic reasons. I lived here at the Algonquin when I first came to New York."

I asked her how it happened that she had moved to New York from London, where I knew she had built an impressive reputation as editor of the *Tatler*, the sophisticated British magazine.

"Let me start from the beginning," she suggested.

"When I graduated from Oxford I never had any thought of becoming an editor. I was interested in writing plays and articles. I was particularly intrigued with writing social snapshots of the rich, but I never had any idea that this would develop into a career. I enjoyed working, but I always felt that I was a writer, and my ambitions lay in that direction.

"When new management took over the fussy, dying *Tatler*, Nigel Dempster, the prominent London journalist, recommended me for the job as editor. I was tenth on the list of candidates, and when I was offered the position, I took it. I always had a sense of fun about the aristocracy. I had come to know that world, and it was mutually agreed by everyone involved that a maverick approach to life among the rich and titled of Great Britain would be the basis of our editorial policy.

LACK OF EXPERIENCE HELPED

"I was completely inexperienced as an editor, but this proved to be a help rather than a hindrance. There was nothing for me to test my judgments against, so there was nothing for me to lose. I was twenty-five when I was named editor of the *Tatler*. My boss gave me a free hand, and I began to recruit my literary friends from Oxford as writers and staff members. I knew that although I received instant support and encouragement from management, I had to produce almost instant results.

"Having trained myself as a playwright and with some knowledge of the theater, I likened bringing out a new magazine to producing a play. As the editor I saw myself as the director of the play, and using that approach, I discovered that I had a repressed executive gene in my personality. Although I worked under enormous pressure,

I found myself having great fun. I loved being a catalyst, bringing people together to publish a magazine. I enjoyed discovering new talent.

"I was becoming an influence in London publishing circles and I got great satisfaction from making things happen. I edited the *Tatler* for four years. During that time circulation grew from twelve thousand to forty thousand copies per month, and advertising increased from fifteen to seventy-five pages per issue.

TIME FOR A CHANGE

"When Gary Bogard sold the *Tatler* to Condé Nast, I decided it was time for a change in life-style, and I resigned to resume my writing career. That didn't last long. I quickly decided that I had made a mistake, because I missed being an editor. Just at that time, my husband, Harold Evans, who had had a long, successful career as editor of the London *Times* and the London Sunday *Times*, had a run-in with Rupert Murdoch, who had recently bought the newspapers. That seemed to be an ideal time for us to take a holiday in Barbados. It was Christmas 1983, and we had no sooner sat down for our first gin and tonic than there was a telephone call for me.

"It was Alex Lieberman, editorial director of Condé Nast Publications. Would I please interrupt my holiday for just one day to come to New York to have lunch with him and Mr. Newhouse, the owner of Condé Nast. I was certain that they would offer me some writing assignments for *Vogue* and a number of other publications, and with Harry's blessing, I left him sitting in the sun, telling him that I would return in forty-eight hours.

"At lunch I learned that they were not interested in giving me writing assignments. They offered me the editorship of *Vanity Fair*. Condé Nast had revived the old *Vanity Fair* a year before, and it was a disaster. They had already fired two editors and were debating whether they should close down the magazine. They had decided that, having accomplished what I had for the *Tatler*, I was the only person who might possibly turn *Vanity Fair* around.

NO TIME TO THINK IT OVER

"This was an interesting dilemma for me. Harry and I had always lived in England and had never given any thought to taking up residence in the United States. Now suddenly an exciting opportunity opened up for me, but what about my husband? I asked Mr. Lieberman and Mr. Newhouse if I could have some time to think it over. No, they wanted an answer immediately. In fact, they wanted me to start work on January first, only a few days away. I had to think quickly. I knew it was a fabulous offer, and that if I wasted time considering, the offer would probably disappear. They would find another editor or make the drastic move of closing down the magazine. I asked to use the telephone and called Harry.

"He insisted that this was a big opportunity for me and that I must accept the offer; I shouldn't worry about him. He was willing to move to the States because, after having had the two top editorships in London for many years, there was nothing left for him in England that was sufficiently challenging to keep him in the U.K. He was certain that he could build a whole new career for himself in the U.S.

"Before the afternoon was over, I had accepted the job of editor of *Vanity Fair.* Harry had agreed that I should stay on in New York and that he would return to London from Barbados to close up our house, settle our affairs, and he would see me in a few weeks. I never went back to Barbados and never returned to London. It was a quick, clean break from the past and a dramatic entrance into the most exciting years of my life."

Tina Brown is a daring young woman who took a risk and won. In half an hour's time she came to a decision to move from England to the United States. There are times when you are not given the luxury of thinking things over. You have to make a decision almost instantaneously, but there are people who know when they're on a roll, and they allow the next throw of the dice to determine the course of their lives. This may or may not be the best way for *you* to make decisions, but Tina Brown is a wonderful example of a woman who grasped an opportunity when it was offered to her—and succeeded.

ANOTHER SUCCESSFUL RISK-TAKER

Joanne Black, senior vice president of marketing for Mastercard is another successful woman who isn't afraid of taking risks. She is a strong believer that making detours, moving laterally, and moving into a number of different jobs over a period of years is the right route to take for a successful career. At least, it was for her.

Joanne was a college dropout in the early sixties. She arrived in New York from a working-class neighborhood in Baltimore, determined to be a successful actress. But after discovering that the struggle for an acting career was not synonymous with eating regularly, and with three meals a day uppermost in her mind, she became a medical secretary, ran a coffee shop, and later worked in a blue-collar bar called the Nancy Whiskey Pub. Always ambitious and always striving to improve herself, she convinced Bristol-Myers to use her as a spokesperson for Clairol on radio and television talk shows.

Her talents began to become apparent at about that time, and Clairol took her on as an assistant marketing manager. That brought her into the Madison Avenue–based world of advertising for the first time. After three years she left to become the first female account executive at Ogilvy & Mather, one of the world's top advertising agencies.

By this time she had developed a confidence in her marketing talents, and she was secure about her ability to keep working. She had no qualms about moving around a lot. So in 1971 she transferred to Bristol-Myers, Clairol's parent company, as a product manager. Within the year she'd jumped again, this time to the Bali Company, as marketing director. When a headhunter for American Express caught up with her in 1976, she was the advertising manager for Celanese Fibers Marketing Company.

NEW YORK BURNOUT

She accepted the job at American Express, but after seven years in senior marketing positions there, Joanne decided that she was ready for another change in her life. She awakened one morning to discover that she was a victim of New York burnout. She had just divorced. She had reached the age of forty. And it was time to get out of the corporate world. She went to San Francisco and opened her own consulting business.

"I was tired of fighting, she said. "I wanted to see what it was like to move to another city and live differently. I liked it, but I admit that I did miss the fight." After a year and a half in her own business, Joanne was ready to come back to the corporate world, and she accepted a position at Mastercard, the nation's number-two bank card company. "I missed that sense of really playing the game in an important way," she says.

Today Joanne Black is one of New York's most successful marketing executives. She is another woman who proves that there are no set rules for pursuing a career. My observation is that her innate talent gave her the courage to make moves and to take risks. She was never worried about losing a job or quitting a job, because she always knew that she had the ability to create another opportunity for herself.

RISK AND SUCCESS

Lisa Specht, a successful Los Angeles attorney, told me, "The most important rule of them all, and in this I am talking from personal experience, is that you must take risks. If you play it safe, you'll never make it. If you don't like your job, then take the risk and find something else you want to do. You'll never be successful in a job you don't like. If anyone were to ask me what was the key to the success I've had thus far in my life, I would have to say that it was due to my willingness to take risks. In law school, I took the toughest elective classes. When I became a lawyer I kept asking for new assignments, even though I knew I wouldn't get a decent night's sleep for two weeks at a time. My advice to young women, then, is to take risks. If you don't, you'll stagnate. And if you stagnate, you'll never have a successful career."

THE JOB IS NOT WHAT YOU THOUGHT IT WOULD BE

Sometimes there is a tremendous gulf between the job that was described to you when you were being interviewed and the job that you actually end up doing nine to five. Your new assignment now appears to be neither as important nor as challenging as you had envisioned it. Don't let this disturb you too much; a job description is really determined in practice, during your early days on the job, not in discussion. And there are things that you can do to tailor your job description to your abilities and expectations.

Once you have definitely determined that your new world is not the one that was first described to you, it is time to take stock of where you are. The job is different from what you expected, but before you jump to conclusions about this new "tragedy" that's come into your life, analyze the situation carefully. It may be different, but is it bad? Is it actually worse than you expected? Think through where this job will take you a year from now, and contrast that with where you might have been if the job were more like it was first described to you. If your projection puts you in an equal or even a better career position, then you are better off leaving things as they are. Conversely, if it appears that you will be worse off, and the job, as you view it, derails your long-range career plans, then don't sit back and give the company endless cooperation. It is time to fight for your rights. You may not want to raise a ruckus, but it is important for you to be perceived as a woman who will take a stand.

You can assert yourself in one of two ways. First, you may be able to manipulate your work responsibilities in such a way that, without even discussing it with anyone, your job will turn out to be exactly as it had been described to you. But if this doesn't work for you, speak up and point out that that's not the job you were hired for. You will be declaring to your boss and to yourself that you are in control of your life and your career. Taking a stand doesn't mean that you shouldn't compromise. Compromises make the world go round, but it is important for everyone to know that you're not a doormat.

HAVE YOU BEEN MANIPULATED?

Suppose you discover that you've been manipulated. Suppose you discover that your boss never had any intention of giving you the job you thought was being offered to you. It is time to take a deep breath and bring the whole situation out into the open. You will then at least know the score and know where you stand. Then you can make your own decision whether to leave or stay on, in the hope that there will be other chances and other jobs that are better for you in the future.

ARE YOU IN OVER YOUR HEAD?

One day you awaken in a cold sweat and ask yourself, "How did I get into this mess? I'm in over my head." In your unswerving drive for a successful career, you had your eye on a new job for a long time; you opted for it, campaigned for it, and finally got it. Now, a few weeks later, you fear that you've made a dreadful mistake. You're not qualified for this job. It requires skills that you don't have. It calls for abilities that are beyond your current level of competence. You're making a damn fool of yourself, everyone is laughing at your feeble attempts to cope, and your boss is looking daggers at you, probably wondering, "How am I going to get rid of her?"

Those are the thoughts that are going through your head as you crawl out of bed to face another day of terror. Has this ever happened to you? If it hasn't, it may one day in the future, so let's look at a few ideas about how to cope with your job when you are convinced that you're in over your head.

First of all, you might be wrong. Your boss isn't an idiot. He or she may know you and your capabilities better than you do yourself. If it wasn't clear to him or her that you could handle this job, you wouldn't have gotten it. Your situation is typical of many people's. Some people have great self-confidence, but many others are less secure. They may underestimate their skills and qualifications, or have some fears about moving up to jobs with which they are unfamiliar. If you fall into this category, you are at a crucial point in your life: you have reached the point at which the die-hard male chauvinists have predicted that you will fall by the wayside. They said that you weren't strong enough to make it to the top, that you didn't have the persistence, the courage, or the know-how to go all the way. Are you going to let them be proved right? I can't believe that you are.

ROGERS' RULES FOR COPING WITH THE FEAR THAT YOU'RE IN OVER YOUR HEAD

1. Don't quit your job. And don't try to solve the problem alone.
2. You need help in deciding what your next move should be. Don't be reluctant to seek it out. Send out an SOS!

3. Start by discussing the problem with your spouse, your lover, your best friend, your mother, your father, or anyone else who knows you and has some knowledge of the business in which you work.

4. If none of these people have any useful advice, go to trusted peers and colleagues, and eventually to your boss.

5. If your colleagues and your boss disagree with your concerns, if they say that you're not in over your head, then you know that you have a psychological rather than an actual problem. Diagnosis: you're better than you think you are.

6. To overcome your insecurity, increase your current skill level by seeking the advice of higher-ups who can give you added insights into your job, by taking courses, by reading about your job and your industry, or by participating in seminars. You were good before, but after all this you'll be a superstar.

7. If your boss agrees that he or she has made a mistake and that you *are* in over your head, ask for advice about how to improve your performance. Ask for help, and tell him or her that you are planning to enhance your skills by starting the kinds of activities outlined above.

8. If your boss feels that you're a lost cause, you still have choices:

   A. Ask for three months to prove yourself.

   B. Ask for your former job.

   C. Ask for a transfer to another department.

   D. If none of these options are available, ask to be dismissed or try to reach an agreement with your boss that you may stay on for a time so that you can look for another job. It's always preferable to start job hunting while you are still on someone's payroll.

If you believe that you are in over your head in your present job and that you might lose your job by confronting the problem, you're still better off looking the problem in the eye. It's better to face up to the situation than to live a life of insecurity with the sword of Damocles dangling over your head day after day.

CAREER STRATEGY BONUS

SUCCESSFUL WOMEN ADVISE YOU ON LAUNCHING AND ADVANCING YOUR CAREER

I interviewed many women for this book, and at some point, I asked them all, "What advice do you have for young women who are about to launch their careers, or, having launched them, aren't sure about what their next moves should be?"

Their answers:

Anne Luther, Schieffelin & Co.: "The first point I would stress is *patience*. You all have the idea that you're going to be hotshot successes overnight. It doesn't work that way. The first five years are going to be tough while you're learning. Yes, it's going to take that long. Second, stay *flexible*. Roll with the punches."

Phyllis Kaminsky, United Nations Information Center: "Don't take yourself too seriously. Retain a sense of humor. Don't worry about little things. Stay cool. Don't put yourself in a position to permit a man to put you down. You won't win all the time. If you're defeated, accept it with dignity."

Lisa Specht, Mannatt, Phelps, Rothenberg, and Philips: "Watch what other people do. Pick out everyone else's best points and try to emulate them. You have to kill your-self. Forget forty-hour weeks. You have to work six days a week, even seven. The first impressions you create are all-important, and it's essential that right from the begin-ning you develop an image as an incredibly hard worker.

Paula Meehan, Redken Hair Products: "Work in an area that is of vital interest to you. If you can find the job that is right for you, then work for less money than you could get in a job you didn't really care about. Stay with it. Don't move around. Work and continuity are important. Use your instincts."

Kathie Berlin, Thomas, Hart & Berlin Productions: "De-cide on the three top jobs you want, and go after them. Start as a secretary if you have to. Learn everything, and then let everyone know that you know everything. If you're smart you'll move up. . . . You should have four or five different jobs before you wind up with the right one."

Louise Sunshine, Louise Sunshine Partners: "Be yourself. Develop your own style, and your own approach to con-ducting business."

Betty Goodwin, freelance writer: "You should do what you love to do. Money is not that important. It is more impor-tant to look forward to every day as another challenging and exciting experience. I feel that you should have pas-sion for your job. Sometimes it doesn't happen at the first moment. Sometimes it develops over a period of time."

Barbara Boyle, Hollywood Film Producer and Studio Ex-ecutive: "Having a title is ego-gratifying, but in the long run it will not help your career unless a certain degree of authority and responsibility come with it. If you really want to get ahead in a business, learn everything about it. Don't be reluctant to say, 'I don't know.' It is preferable to giving someone a superficial observation on a subject with which you're not familiar. You are fortunate because, being a woman, you are in touch with your emotions and your instincts, which men have been forced by society to submerge. This gives you attributes that, coupled with intellectual achievement, can cause women to become great leaders in whatever field they choose."

Kate Ford, Ford Model Agency: "When you get out of school, don't jump into the first job that comes along. Look around, talk to lots of people, and take time to check out the marketplace before you come to a decision. When you finally get a job, study the company and look at all the other positions in the company that might be available to you. Set your eyes ahead. Money should never be your first consideration. Once you find a job that you're sure you can do well, the money will come to you. Take any job that is even related to what you want to do. Typing or even sweeping the floor is okay, if that's what it takes to get your foot in the door."

ROGERS' RULES FOR ADVANCING YOUR CAREER

1. Be persistent. Don't be deterred by roadblocks.
2. Develop drive and self-discipline.
3. Put in the hours.
4. Think ahead about knowledge you will require for future success. Then get it.
5. Learn where the power is.
6. Learn to manage your time.
7. Be assertive in your relationships with your peers and your boss.

8. Find a mentor. Or, better yet, find a number of mentors with different areas of expertise.
9. Develop your network of contacts and sharpen your networking skills.
10. Be alert to new opportunities, and be flexible enough to see how new options can help you to reach your goal.
11. Don't be afraid to take a calculated risk.

6

Managing Your Boss

The title of this chapter probably appears paradoxical to you, but it shouldn't. Bosses can be influenced; bosses can be managed. I certainly do not mean to imply that you can change your boss from an unreasonable monster into a model manager, but you can definitely try to change a boss's attitude and his or her behavior toward you.

From the moment you leave your home in the morning until you open your front door in the evening, your boss is the most important person in your business life. Your boss is the person who, at this early stage in your career, will determine the level of success you will achieve, at least in the short term, while you remain a subordinate. (It's clear that your boss may just as easily be a woman as a man. I will alternate between *he* and *him* and *she* and *her* in this chapter to make the writing evenhanded.) Your ability and competence are important up to a point, but equally important is his perception of you, both as an employee and as a person. He is in a position to evaluate your performance. He can recommend you for a salary increase, or reject your request for one. He can recommend that you be promoted, or make a single well-aimed unkind remark that will doom your chances of ever getting a better position in your present company, or that might even lead to your dismissal.

Your boss can help you or hurt you. Worse yet, he can ignore you. Your boss holds the power of life and death over your career in his hands. Yet it has always been puzzling to me that most people accept the status quo in their relationships with their bosses, which is usually a nonexistent relationship: he is who and what he is, they are who and what they are, and that's the way it is. "Let's hope," they say, "that everything turns out for the best. Let's hope that we're compatible. I won't like it if I get fired, but I'll get along. I can always get another job, and in the meantime, I'll live on unemployment."

Does this sound cavalier, uncaring? Please believe that many, many people go through their lives and their careers with this attitude. They simply stay out of the boss's way, because that's how to stay out of trouble.

My advice to you is to take a more active role in your relationship with your boss. If you accept my premise that your boss is the most important person in your business life, you must also accept the idea that unless you are fortunate enough to have a perfect boss—and that is *highly* unlikely—you should not just accept or put up with the relationship you currently have with him.

CHANGING FOR THE BETTER

So let's look at your boss and determine how you can improve your relationship with him. And how that improved relationship will be another step forward in the enhancement of your career.

First, as I said, do not accept the status quo. You can change, you can adapt, and although it may be difficult to believe, you can also influence your boss's behavior for the better. And this won't just make him a nicer guy to be around. The kinds of changes I have in mind have one primary objective: the enhancement of your career, a better position, and more money for *you*.

You start by asking yourself, "What steps can I take to change my boss's behavior patterns—and my own—that will help me to succeed?" But before you can answer that question, you must first study your boss, get to know him better, and then study yourself. When you have better insights into the personalities and habits of both yourself and your boss, you will be in a stronger position to evaluate your present relationship with him and to map out a plan to improve it.

Get to know your boss's work habits, his idiosyncrasies, his weaknesses, and his strengths. Look at your own work habits and determine how they fit in with his, and any areas in which the two of you may be in conflict. If she doesn't like to face the problems of the day until she's had her first cup of coffee, don't throw a long list of questions or reminders at her before she sits down at her desk. Be sensitive to her needs. Put yourself in her shoes, and work with her, so that you help rather than hinder her.

If she is given to long monologues, hold your tongue. Don't interrupt her. Every time you interrupt her, you annoy her, and your relationship with her deteriorates.

I was a guest on Larry King's radio show one night and was voicing my views on how to manage your boss, when Larry suddenly asked, "But Henry, isn't that apple-polishing?" I agreed that it was, and then I continued, "How did apple-polishing get such bad press?" I answered my own question. "It probably stems from our early schooldays, when we all used to snicker at the kid who brought an apple to his teacher. We called him a sissy because he was trying to ingratiate himself with the person who gave out the grades. By this time," I told Larry and his audience, "we should all realize that apple-polishing is something to be admired, not vilified. If we could trace the history of that kid who brought an apple for the teacher, we would probably discover that he got an A on his paper when he might have deserved only a B, and that he went on to have a very successful career—not only because he had intelligence and talent, but because of his ability to ingratiate himself with people." By this time we should be sufficiently well-informed to know what makes the business world go round, and to realize that apple-polishing pays both short-term and long-term dividends. It costs nothing to be nice to people. And even though you may collect nothing in return, we all know that the judicious use of honey gets you much farther in this world than a dose of vinegar.

BE A BETTER SUBORDINATE AND HE WILL BE A BETTER BOSS

Once you come to understand your boss a bit better than you do now, it is time to plan and implement a program that will help you to be a better subordinate and him to become a better boss. Yes, it can happen. People do change for the better, but as I said earlier, *you* have to take full responsibility for making your double-barreled improvement plan work, and the bonus is that if you can overcome the hurdles your boss presents to you, it will become comparatively easy for you to understand and deal with anyone in the organization.

Boss problems are not only among the most common of all the perplexing, delicate situations you'll face in the development of your career, they're also some of the most difficult to solve. I am very sensitive to boss problems, because over the years a number of very talented women have left our employ. I discovered later that the reason for their departure was that they found me too difficult to work for. I genuinely believe that I'm very easy to work for. I am demanding, I tend to be a perfectionist, but I never ask more of other people than I ask of myself. However, I obviously don't see myself as my associates see me, because my confidantes at Rogers & Cowan tell me that I am regarded as intimidating and impossible to please.

But my opinion of myself as a boss is unimportant. What is important is the way I'm perceived by my subordinates. I am saddened that a number of talented women have left us, because I'm confident that if they'd discussed their problems with me, we could have arrived at a compromise that would have been to our mutual advantage. I am probably the difficult boss that I am reputed to be, but I am willing to listen. And I'm willing to learn. I believe that most bosses are willing to listen, but many employees are too timid and too insecure to talk out their problems with their employers. It is easier for them to walk away and get another job, with no guarantee that the next boss will be any better than the one they just left. I remember a friend once telling me, "Don't divorce your wife unless you're guaranteed that the next one will be better." The same goes for bosses.

BOSSES AREN'T PERFECT . . .

People sometimes don't understand that even though their bosses are in command positions, they are certainly not perfect. They have their faults like everyone else, and like all human beings they can be handled, managed, and manipulated—for the benefit of all concerned. However, on behalf of bosses, I say with great humility that, although I am willing to point a finger at myself and my managerial peers, I must also point my finger at you, the employee.

Before you throw up your hands in frustration at the manner in which your boss treats you, take a long hard look at yourself. Just as I admit that I don't see myself as my employees see me, so too there is a good chance that when your boss looks at you, he doesn't see the person you see when you look in the mirror.

. . . AND NEITHER ARE EMPLOYEES

Look at yourself through your boss's eyes. This is difficult to do, because it's difficult for any of us to separate our public selves from our egos. If you make a conscious effort, however, to see yourself through the eyes of your boss, you may see another you, and you may begin to understand more readily why you and your boss could be having problems with each other. This objective point of view will be helpful in improving your relationship with the person who is responsible for your biweekly paycheck.

You may be one of the fortunate few who have no complaints about her boss, but if you do have complaints, your first move should be to analyze them to determine their legitimacy. Do you have a good reason to be discontented? Are *you* too demanding? Are *you* too critical? If you compare your boss with your husband, your lover, or your best male friend, do the boss's faults loom much larger than theirs? Before I begin to give you recommendations on how you can try to improve the relationship, first make certain that your problems are genuine, not imaginary.

And if there are real problems, don't automatically assume that you are faultless. Maybe you would like your employer to have different work habits, a different personality, but did you ever thing that *your boss* might feel the same way about *you?*

If after all this you've decided that you would like to improve your relationship with your boss because it will help to advance your career, as well as making your job more pleasant and gratifying on a day to day basis, it is time for me to spell out a number of useful strategies that will help you to succeed in your plan.

In the hundreds of conversations I've had with women about their careers, certain boss-related problems kept reappearing. I will deal with them, because it is most likely that your problems are included in the subjects I'm about to cover. And you should also pay attention to the problems that don't apply to you now, because you may have a new boss next month or next year and discover that one of these situations is complicating your life.

YOU AND YOUR BOSS DON'T COMMUNICATE

I used to worry a lot about the manner in which I conveyed information. I was concerned about whether it was better for me to write a long memo, a short memo, or call for a meeting; whether to try to convey my thoughts in an informal atmosphere outside the office; whether to do it early in the morning, late in the afternoon, or over the morning coffee break. There never seemed to be a right time, so I ultimately decided that I was starting the process of communicating with an incorrect premise. My decisions were based on what was right for *me*, not what was right for the person with whom I wished to communicate.

From that moment on, I changed my approach. I decided that if the information I wished to convey was to be properly received, understood, and acted upon, I would have to tailor my communications methods to the needs, habits, and style of each potential recipient.

Even if you believe you and your boss communicate very well, I am sure there's room for improvement. So let's first explore the way in which you presently communicate, and then see how you can initiate changes that will put you in an even stronger position.

TWO KINDS OF BOSSES

You can usually divide bosses into two categories: readers and listeners. Have you ever thought in those terms before? Now is the time to look at your boss in this new light and decide whether she prefers to communicate in person or on paper.

If she is a reader, she will prefer to have you communicate with her in memo form. The problem may be that she has never thought of telling you that she's a reader, and that is why you may have had problems getting her to pay attention to what you're saying. Do her eyes seem to wander when you talk to her? Does she fidget in her chair? Does she impatiently walk around the office? Think about how she reacts. If her actions are similar to those I've just described, try saying, "Excuse me, would you prefer that I put all this in memo form? Then, once you think about it, you can get back to me about what our next step should be." If she reacts positively to this suggestion, you may be well on your way to solving your communications problem.

Many people, especially people who have to read a lot of memos, believe that in most circumstances the ideal length for a business memo is one paragraph and that in *no* circumstances should it be more than a single page. And if you've written a report that of necessity is many pages and has numerous attachments, they would suggest you write a brief summary or précis as an introduction.

But your boss may be a listener, not a reader. Look for clues to determine whether this might be your problem. If he doesn't respond to your memos, that is a definite clue. If he just glances at a report you've spent many days preparing, tosses it aside, and says to you, "Just give me the gist of it," that is another clue.

Faced with a boss who reacts like this, don't hand her a report with any expectation that she'll read it. First, cut the length of your report—cut, cut, *cut.* The length of your memos may intimidate her, and this reaction will only result in her becoming annoyed with you. Try a one-paragraph report, a page at most. Once you've pared the report, present it to her—orally. *Tell* her, don't read to her, the principle points covered in your report or memo. Then, after the two of you have thoroughly discussed the subject, hand her your report. "Just for the record," you can say to her, knowing full well that she will never bother to read it. Then why bother to write it? "For the record" means just that: she will have a copy in her files, and you will have a copy in yours. If the subject ever comes up again, or if a misunderstanding arises over who said what, you'll both have it on the record.

YOUR BOSS WON'T DELEGATE AUTHORITY TO YOU

This is a complaint I hear all the time. Your boss holds everything close to his chest, he believes that unless he does something himself, it won't get done, and he stands over your shoulder second-guessing you all day long. Does such behavior sound familiar to you? First, let me admit that your boss's behavior is inexcusable, and it proves that he is not a good executive. But he's still your boss, and you may be able to influence his behavior.

Why does he act in such an ineffective manner? Doesn't he realize that he could accomplish much more and get more important results for himself and the company if he'd just let you get on with your job? His problems can be summed up in one word: fear. He is afraid that you won't do the job as well as he can do it, or in the same way he does it. Also, he may have some fear of taking on the new responsibilities that could become available to him if he'd stop doing your job for you. He is comfortable doing your job. It's a cinch for him. It doesn't present a challenge, and he doesn't want to face up to new challenges. This is a terrible indictment of your boss, but once you realize what motivates him, it will be possible for you to deal more effectively with the problem.

What can you do about it? You can get him to turn over certain areas of responsibility to you as a result of changes in your own behavior.

ROGERS' RULES FOR GETTING YOUR BOSS TO DELEGATE AUTHORITY TO YOU

1. Try to anticipate his questions and his needs. If you do something before he asks you to do it, you're on your way to a salary increase.
2. Give her the answers before he asks the questions.
3. Show him that you're aware of all the problems, and that you are already thinking of possible solutions.

4. Do things for her that she would normally do herself. She'll soon discover that there's no need to concern herself with these matters. You are proving your worth.
5. Make recommendations to him about courses of action he might take that he hasn't thought of himself. Bosses don't think of everything and don't always make correct decisions. I know.

All this will certainly not change overnight the habit of not delegating authority, but it's a good beginning. I'm confident that if you consistently act in ways that spotlight the changes in your own behavior, you will soon be able to see changes on his side that will let you do your job more effectively and will simultaneously help your boss become a better executive.

I'll conclude this section by telling you a little secret: your boss will never know what's happening to him. And it's to your advantage *not* to tell him. Let him think that it's all his own idea. He will think that the two of you have become a great team, and you will have achieved your objective.

YOUR BOSS DOESN'T GIVE YOU ENOUGH DIRECTION

This is another complaint I hear constantly, and I give an answer that most people don't like. You probably won't like it, either. Why should he give you direction? Are you a trainee, an intern? If you are new to the work world, you should be receiving direction and guidance.

Unfortunately, many people with a certain kind of expertise simply assume the same level of expertise in others. If your boss assumes expertise that you just don't have yet, you'll have to ask for guidance, either from him or from your more experienced colleagues. Someone, after all, has to show you the ropes. However, many of the women who complained to me about their boss's inattention to guidance were in management positions—lower, middle, or upper—and they really shouldn't *need* day to day direction.

Once you've been in a job for a couple of years and have a promotion or two under your belt, you should be sufficiently knowledgeable about your job that your boss doesn't have to tell you what to do and how and when to do it. If you've had some job experience, part of what you're being paid for is the business judgment and decision-making ability you've acquired. You may not see yourself as a leader or a self-sufficient worker who can take over total responsibility for a project. But if you admit that you lack confidence in your judgment, you must also realize that you cannot move up to a higher management level until you gain that confidence. Suggestion: to achieve confidence (with training wheels), mention your decisions to your boss before you act on them.

But are you in over your head? If you think that you might be a living example of the Peter Principle, i.e., the theory that people rise to the level of their own incompetence, then be sure to recognize it before your boss does. Seek help from trusted colleagues, but *not* from your boss. You can always find people in any organization who are willing to help others, and if you ask for help and indicate your appreciation, they will continue to help you until you have raised your skills to the required level of competence.

FEEDBACK AND COACHING

There is a difference between expecting your boss to give you direction and looking to him for feedback and coaching. When you expect direction from the boss, you are waiting for him to teach you the basics, the elementary principles of your job. If you have been working for a number of years, you should have already learned such things. Taking direction is the equivalent of taking lessons from your local piano teacher, who will teach you how to read music, how to place your fingers on the keys, and how to use the foot pedal. Getting feedback and coaching is the equivalent of being a student at the Juilliard School in New York and being tutored by some of the finest artists in the world in the most sophisticated techniques and nuances that will help you to become a concert pianist.

YOUR BOSS DOESN'T PRAISE YOU FOR YOUR ACCOMPLISHMENTS

Your life has changed enormously since your college days. Way back then, you or your parents *paid* for you to be educated. Some of you received superior grades, most received average grades, and some of you just skimmed by, but you all graduated with the same piece of parchment in your hands—a diploma.

Did anyone heap accolades on you for receiving a diploma? I doubt it. A few of you did receive pats on the back for being selected Phi Beta Kappa or graduating summa cum laude, but no one is complimented just because she received a BA or BS or whatever letters follow your name at this point in your life. A degree is just a sign of competence, not unusual achievement. In school, and in your early career days, no one is going to praise you for competence. Competence is what you paid to gain in college. Competence in your job is what you are *being paid for*. Don't expect to be praised for it.

However, you should be praised for extraordinary achievements. Try to look at the whole thing from that perspective. How many times have you been annoyed with your boss because he didn't compliment you for something you had done? Quite often, I'm sure. Now think back. How many truly extraordinary accomplishments are we talking about? Very few. Right? Very, very few. From this point of view, your boss may not be as insensitive to excellence as you've always thought.

ROGERS' RULES FOR GETTING PRAISE FOR YOUR ACCOMPLISHMENTS

1. Evaluate your performance from your boss's perspective. Do you expect a pat on the back for doing what you're being paid to do, or for something really beyond the call of duty?
2. If you discover that you've been expecting compliments for a merely competent performance, it's time to change your expectations.
3. Don't assume that your boss knows everything that you're doing. He has other things and other people on his mind, and your efforts are much more significant to you than they are to him.
4. Let him know, either by telling him or in a memo, what you're doing over and above the routine work you're being paid for.
5. If compliments are important to you, put forth the extra effort that will result in extraordinary performance.

COMING TO TERMS WITH A TEMPERAMENTAL BOSS

No one, not even a CEO, has a divine right to temper tantrums. Temper tantrums reflect bad manners—they are also bad business. But everyone has a flash point. Some of us explode more easily than others; some can take an incredible amount of pressure before the detonation is touched off, and others seem to be on the verge of a temper tantrum during every working hour. If your boss explodes occasionally, and then cools down almost as quickly as he heats up, you may want to weather these infrequent storms and just accept them as part of his personality. If, on the other hand, his outbursts are frequent and appear to be uncontrollable, and if it is affecting your own job performance, there may be something you can do about it.

You must acknowledge the fact that your boss may not be able to change this aspect of his behavior. But you may be able to change your reaction to his cyclonic behavior, and therein lies the simplest solution to your problem. If you can train yourself to listen to and watch his choleric outbursts without emotion, without resentment, and with complete detachment, you'll have it made. The bottom line: don't take it personally. It's *his* problem, not yours.

Start with the premise that this poor, excitable, temperamental man, who happens to be your boss, has a serious emotional problem. He's sick, and just as you would never be resentful or impatient with a person who had cancer or pneumonia or heart trouble, you should have compassion and empathy for him. Important: this is *not* a subject for you to discuss with him. He would probably be furious with you if you said to him, "I know that you have an emotional problem and I'm going to help you." A person in his condition not only would resent your presumption, he probably isn't even aware of the fact that he has a problem.

Your attitude toward him—of which he should be unaware—should be something like this: "This sad gentleman is suffering from an illness, and I feel sorry for him, but I won't allow him to aggravate me or upset me with his emotional pyrotechnics. I'll learn how to handle this myself, and I'll remain calm in the midst of the storm."

I admit that this may not be an easy attitude to acquire and to project consistently. But if you make a serious effort you may find that it can be done. And you will also find that you'll be able to ride out his emotional storms without their affecting your own emotional state. However, no one has to put up with a nine-to-five, five-day-a-week ogre. If he's really that bad, do yourself a favor and get out from under his supervision—if necessary, by looking for a new job.

WHY DOES HE GET ANGRY?

Did you ever wonder why he blows up so often? It may be that he lacks confidence in the people who work for him, people who are supposed to be helping him in his career. He gets panicky when it appears to him that something is not working as it should, and automatically, or unconsciously or subconsciously, he starts yelling, because he genuinely believes that yelling will help to get everything straightened out. Important: maybe he has a justifiable beef. Have you made a mistake, let him down, or disappointed him in some way? Look at the situation through *his* eyes, and to make sure you've done nothing to incur his wrath.

ROGERS' RULES FOR NOT LETTING YOUR BOSS GET YOU DOWN

1. Don't try to avoid her. In fact, try to spend more time with her, helping her and trying to anticipate situations that may cause problems farther down the road.
2. If you make a mistake, tell him about it before he finds out about it for himself. Forget about small mistakes. He will probably never notice them.
3. When she explodes—and she will—try listening to her.
4. Let him finish his tirade without interrupting.
5. After she has wound down, if you believe you have a logical side to your story, present your case objectively and confidently, without being apologetic.
6. Don't argue with him, and don't let the level of your voice rise to meet his.
7. Try to understand his criticism, and if there is any justification for his anger, give him the benefit of the doubt. Agree with him. By validating his complaint instead of fighting it, you will have left him with nothing more to yell about, and he will have forgotten all about the incident the next day.

You may disagree with my approach. You may think, "Why should I agree with her if she's wrong? Why should I let her get away with it?" The problem with that kind of attitude is that it will lead you into a sparring match with him. And whether you win or lose, you will end up in the same highly charged emotional state that he is in. When it's all over, you'll be flushed with anger, you'll have an ulcerlike pain in your stomach, and you will say to yourself, "I can't stand this any longer. I'm going to quit my job."

I'm certain that my way is better. You remain above the fray, you stay cool, and you keep saying to yourself, "This poor guy has an emotional problem and I'm not going to let it get me down." But remember, you're not the Red Cross, and you're free to seek a better job opportunity elsewhere.

YOUR BOSS HAS NO TIME FOR YOU

You have good reason to be disturbed if your boss's unwillingness to spend time with you has a detrimental effect on your performance. You're certain that you can improve your productivity immeasurably if he'd just give you a little extra attention. In fact, this is probably the root of your problem. You feel that you need more of his attention, and it's obvious that he disagrees with you. This *might* be a good sign. Your boss might think that you're doing fine without his extra input, and he's reluctant to tamper with excellence—the old, "If it ain't broke, don't fix it" philosophy. However, his reluctance to spend time with you might signal a rift or misunderstanding of which you're unaware. In fact, it's more likely that trouble is brewing, and if so, it's necessary for you to take action *now*.

Trouble may arise for one of two reasons. First, your boss may not regard you or your job as being of sufficient importance for him to devote any time to. If that's the case, you should grit your teeth, take a deep breath, and try to make an appointment to see him. If he is unwilling to go along with this, you must resort to a more subtle approach. Time your movements so that you happen to meet him "by chance" in the hall, the elevator, or the company cafeteria, or perhaps in the parking lot as he is arriving in the morning or leaving in the evening.

Once you've nabbed him—what do you say? Tell him that you want to do your best, and that you'd appreciate a little of his time to discuss some questions you have about your responsibilities. Maybe he'll be impressed by your initiative and will decide to help you achieve your goals. Maybe he'll ignore your request or tell you that there's nothing he can do to help you. At this point, you haven't lost a thing; you're just back where you started. At least you know where you stand, and you can make a more informed decision about whether to stay where you are and wait for better days or move on to another job somewhere else.

There may be another reason why your boss is giving you short shrift. If he used to have time for you but he no longer does, you may have a different problem. You may have disappointed or dissatisfied him in some way, and he has consequently withdrawn his tutelage. Maybe the hours he has spent with you have been unproductive or unpleasant. He might feel that you've been wasting his time. This may be unpleasant for you to think about, but it might be the truth, and you may have to face up to it. Again, asking him for an appointment to discuss the situation is the way to go.

CONVINCE HIM THAT HE'LL PROFIT BY INVESTING TIME IN YOU

It's important for you to understand that your boss is striving to be successful too. He probably works eight, ten, or twelve hours a day, and he must use his time productively. If he spends time with other people and not with you, it must mean that he thinks time with you is not in his or the company's best interests. You must convince him otherwise.

Tell him that if you've disappointed him or let him down, you'd like another chance to prove your worth to him. Tell him that you're ambitious, and that his opinion of you is very important to you. He may deny that there is anything wrong between you. He may be telling the truth, or he may be lying, but at least you have it out in the open and he knows that you care. You certainly haven't endangered your relationship with him, and you may have even enhanced it.

If he hasn't given you more time because he genuinely hasn't had the time or he's never regarded you as sufficiently important, you have now brought yourself to his attention, and you must step up your efforts to impress him.

ROGERS' RULES FOR GETTING YOUR BOSS TO SPEND TIME WITH YOU

1. Try to convince her that spending time with you is a good investment for her. Your success will reflect well upon her expert coaching, and you'll enhance her department.
2. Try to convince him that by teaching you certain skills, he'll save time by being able to delegate more, and more effectively, to you.
3. Don't waste her time; if others in the organization can answer your questions, take their time, not hers.
4. Don't ask him to do your thinking for you.
5. Before you meet with her, prepare an agenda, keeping in mind that the topics for discussion must be in her interest as well as your own.
6. Make sure that you don't overstay your welcome. Before the meeting starts, ask him how much time he has available for you.
7. Make sure that when the meeting ends, she is better informed that when it started.

By following these rules you may find that your boss will see and appreciate that spending extra time with you is to his advantage. Debbie Myers, my acquaintance at the Interdevelopment Bank in Washington, D.C., has the right idea. "About once a month I set up a meeting with my boss," Debbie says. "I bring him up to date on what I've been doing. I also give him my observations about what's going on in our department, and in other departments as well. I never ask him for anything for myself. Instead, I try to act as a source of information for him. I never realized whether he was or was not interested in the information I gave him until the other day. Then he scolded me for not having brought him a piece of news as soon as I heard it, rather than waiting for my regular meeting with him, which was almost a month later. Now I know better."

YOUR BOSS WON'T MAKE THE DECISIONS

You may be one of the many people who are frustrated and unhappy because their bosses seem incapable of making decisions. You may see this indecisiveness as inefficiency, laziness, or just plain carelessness. But I don't really believe that. It is much more likely that your boss's reluctance to make commitments stems from something more complex.

A common cause of indecisiveness is fear. Your boss may be afraid to make a decision because he has long since concluded that as long as he does nothing, he stays out of trouble. If he makes a decision and he's wrong, he'll have let himself in for all kinds of problems. He has learned to survive by not sticking his neck out.

If your boss puts off getting back to you on important issues, if you have difficulty in getting him to make decisions about whether or not to proceed on a new project, you are in an untenable position. You are charged with the responsibility of getting a job done, and he is preventing you from doing it.

And although fear is the primary reason that some bosses are procrastinators, your boss may be acting—or failing to act—for different reasons. It may be that your project is on the bottom of his priority list. Does she make decisions for other people but not for you? That could be a clue for you to study. Also consider the possibility that she won't give you a decision because she's still waiting for a decision from *her* boss. Maybe a higher-up is the villain. Finally, your boss may just be an ornery person with a sadistic streak who won't give you the green light to proceed simply because she knows that she can frustrate you by hanging you up. (Yes, there are people like that.)

What to do? There are many steps you can take to solve your problem, but you'll find it helpful in planning your attack if you first discover the reason your boss procrastinates. Study him; observe the way he acts with other people. Once you've made up your mind about the cause of his indecisiveness, you are in a better position to take countermeasures. Here are some suggestions:

ROGERS' RULES FOR COPING WITH A PROCRASTINATING BOSS

1. Try *not* waiting for him. If the consequences of making the wrong decision aren't grave, make your own decisions and see if he stops you. Maybe he really wants you to relieve him of the responsibility.
2. Inform her of deadlines, and if she still doesn't move, proceed on your own. What can you lose?

3. Give him the pros and cons of various scenarios. Maybe he doesn't know the answer, and the information and insights that you supply might just be the ammunition he needs to make a decision.
4. Give her your recommendations about what her decision should be. Some bosses just have to be pushed. If she is the kind who is paralyzed by fear, she is likely to approve your recommendation, because then she can blame you if something goes wrong.
5. Maybe you have not been clear enough in your explanation of the matter on which you need a decision. If you spell it out simply, it will make it easier for him to give you a response.

YOUR BOSS IS JUST PLAIN UNREASONABLE

Most people run up against a truly troublesome boss at some point in their careers. If you are suffering with an unbearable boss and are helpless to do anything about it, there is one small consolation. Michael Lombardo, a research psychologist at the Center for Creative Leadership in Greensboro, North Carolina, says that there are a few rewards you can reap if you are able to survive a monster boss.

"You can learn how to do things better by watching someone else do them wrong," he says. According to Lombardo, you can learn valuable lessons in how *not* to treat people. And dealing with a bad boss helps to build character—no kidding. Lombardo explains this seemingly contradictory phenomenon. "The situations that develop you the most are often the most stressful. Having a bad boss is on a par with surviving a takeover, or taking on a division that's losing money and turning it around. It's considered a feather in your cap if you can cope with a bad boss." This explanation might be difficult for you to accept, but as an alternative to quitting your job in this kind of situation it sounds like good advice.

Don't kid yourself by thinking that your unbearable boss will change: he probably won't. His behavior patterns were established many years ago, and it is unlikely that they will ever improve. His flaws are part of his personality, and there is probably nothing that you or anyone else can do about that. How are you going to cope with this dreadful person? You have two choices: quit your job, or take the advice of Stuart Margulies, a New York City psychologist who suggests that you approach the problem in a state of "mental preparation."

"What you say to yourself is important," says Dr. Margulies. "You may be attacking yourself, calling yourself names like 'apple-polisher' and 'toady.' You can choose instead to see your predicament as part of your corporate responsibility. You can give yourself the challenge of learning to manage your boss, as you would a difficult client."

Dr. Margulies also warns against "the attitude that, since you've got twenty-two years in the pension fund, you've got to put up with the boss for another ten. Instead, think what you can do to minimize the pain." His suggestions: "Tell yourself . . . that your goal over the next three months will be to reduce your contact with him by twenty-five percent. Giving yourself a positive goal is a way to avoid the feeling of helplessness, which makes things worse."

Coping with an unreasonable boss is a problem that doesn't have easy answers. My only suggestion is that you avoid him as much as possible, but if that gives you no relief, walking out on him may be the only solution.

Earlier I dealt with the subject of people relations, your ability to get people to relate to you as well as your ability to relate to people. Managing your boss calls for the ultimate in people relations skills. It can make the difference between a happy and an unhappy workday, and even the difference between a successful and an unsuccessful career.

Keep in mind that the onus is on you. It's your responsibility to relate to your boss; it's your responsibility to understand him; it's your responsibility to put yourself in his shoes and look at your relationship from his point of view and his perspective.

Is that fair? you ask. Of course it's not. Whoever said that the business world was fair? It's unfair. If he doesn't relate to you or to his other subordinates his sins may catch up with him one day, and he could find himself out of a job—but don't bet on it, and don't wait for it to happen. Don't worry about him and his faults, worry about yourself. Think about your future, about where you are going to be a year or five years from now. Each boss you have will be a challenge to you. Your next boss might be better than this one, or he might be worse. Don't let your career depend on your boss. Your career depends on you, and if you learn how to manage your present boss, it will help you to manage the next one even better.

7

What's Sex Got to Do With It?

If you are just starting out in the business world, or if you've already launched your career, you should accept that the chemistry that exists between men and women is and always will be a part of your business life. Consciously or unconsciously, you transmit sexual signals to men, and they send them out to you too. How these signals are interpreted on both sides may have significant impact on the development of your career.

You will discover, if you haven't already done so, that the subject of sex is one of the more difficult problems you will have to confront in the pursuit of a career. It is easy for me to tell you how to manage your boss, dress for success, have good manners, relate to your co-workers, and broaden your horizons, but when it comes to sex in the workplace, there are no established, ready-made rules. There are no agreed-upon patterns of behavior. Each successful business executive, each psychologist, mentor, writer, and business consultant has a different point of view.

I have my own, but I am not urging you to follow it. I will tell you about the hazards and the advantages, the pluses and the minuses. I will report to you what other women advise, and finally I will make my own observations. At that point it will be up to you to make your own decision as to whether there will be a relationship between your career and your sex life.

You will have to make your own decision because it is impossible to reach a consensus. There are women who say absolutely not, others who say go ahead, and still others who say yes—with many warnings. Let me give you a few examples.

Many women executives have strong feelings on the subject of no sex in the workplace. Paula Meehan, president of Redken Laboratories, says, "I don't believe in sex in the workplace because it has a distracting influence. . . . You can't pay attention to both in business."

Ms. Meehan makes a strong point in stating that an office affair is a distracting influence on a woman who is devoted to building a career. Many women agree with this, because they believe that a certain degree of self-denial is essential in the pursuit of a successful career. Others, however, believe just as strongly that career women can lead normal lives—they consider sex with colleagues from work part of a normal life—and still rise to the top of the career ladder.

It really comes down to who you are, where your primary interests lie, and whether you can successfully juggle more than one ball in the air. If you are devoted to your career one hundred percent and are the kind of person who must devote your life to only one subject in order to achieve your goal, then you have no choice. You must banish the thought of ever having an affair, casual or serious, with a co-worker. There are other women who derive great satisfaction from being able to successfully juggle career, leisure time, love, and sex simultaneously. I neither approve nor disapprove of this kind of life-style. I am pointing out to you once again that you have many choices to make.

Of course, you had these same choices during your college years, but the consequences of your decisions then were not as serious as they are today, when your career is at stake. If a casual affair with a fellow student broke up with resultant acrimony and gossip, it is unlikely that it had a permanent damaging effect on your life. In your present position such an incident could result in a temporary or even permanent setback to your career.

Paula Meehan delivers a grim warning, one that would effectively derail most kinds of self-destructive behavior. But sex has always been a complicated issue, and the recent influx of women into the predominantly male business environment hasn't made it any simpler. Today 44 percent of the work force is female. Men and women are thrown together for hours at a time; they must work together as a team, sometimes under "trench warfare" conditions; they may sometimes have to make out-of-town trips together; and the male-female chemistry that I mentioned earlier will, from time to time, create a tremendous attraction. The unfortunate paradox: if you're putting in the hours on your job that success in business demands, and if you really can't stomach the local singles scene, the office may be the only place you're likely to meet people who could become your friends and social contacts.

A no-win situation? That depends on the way you choose to handle it. Let's say that a single man is transferred to your office from corporate headquarters in another city. He works in a different division of the company, but you meet in the parking lot one day, strike up a conversation, and discover that you share several common interests. He suggests that you get together for a game of tennis, a Chinese dinner, or a stroll through the local art museum. You've been working hard for the last few weeks, and you really need a break.

Okay, let's stop the tape here and analyze the situation. If you're both single and uninvolved, and if you don't report to him and he doesn't report to you, and if there's mutual attraction, it's pretty difficult to turn him down. Your standard of professional behavior—and, presumably, his—would be sufficient to keep most of the office tongues from wagging, and anyway, he's only asked you for a date, not an instant commitment to elope. You have one more thing to consider before you accept, but it's a major consideration, and one that you should think through carefully and honestly.

What if this date leads to the love affair of your dreams . . . and then that wonderful affair for some reason comes to an end? Can you handle running into him on the elevator day after day, going to staff meetings where he might be in attendance, seeing him at company social functions with other women? In fact, if you both continue to work in the same industry, even if you're later employed by different companies, you and he might cross paths for years, for the rest of your business life. If you truly think, despite the clear warnings of some very savvy business people and every grain of your own common sense, that you could handle the short-term and long-term potential difficulties of an office affair, then maybe you should accept that invitation.

SOMETIMES IT ALL WORKS OUT . . .

And sometimes these friendships evolve into lifelong commitments. Carla Schalman Friedman is an account executive at Rogers & Cowan. She graduated from USC in the spring of 1979 and joined the firm as a trainee that July. She took a gamble on an office affair, and now she is married to Sandy Friedman, a long-time senior vice president in our company.

"I came to Rogers & Cowan because of Sandy's help," Carla told me one day. "When I decided that I would like to go into public relations, a friend of mine telephoned Sandy and arranged for me to meet with him. He took me in to meet with Paul Bloch, and I went to work almost immediately.

"One day at a company softball game, Sandy asked me to have dinner with him, but I said no. I was involved with another man at the time, and I also turned him down because I felt that it would adversely affect our working relationship. My resolve didn't last too long. When Sandy drove me home late that afternoon he again asked to take me out. This time I agreed, and I took him to a party that same night that I'd been invited to.

"I must confess that that first night I knew I was on a date with someone who was very special. We both broke off the relationships we had with other people, and a few weeks later we were going steady. I felt strange going to the office every morning. Sandy and I tried to act as casually as we could, but people sensed very quickly that something was going on between us, and the general consensus was that we were a 'cute' couple."

There were a few snide remarks passed about Carla getting ahead in her career because she was sleeping with Sandy. She says, "I replied to those cracks by saying that if I wanted to sleep my way to success, I wouldn't do it with a vice president, I'd go right to the top. My answer seemed to stop any further gossip. I knew that I didn't have to impress the gossipy women in the secretarial pool, but I did have to impress upper management with my talents as a professional, not as someone's girlfriend.

"In January of 1980 Sandy and I began to share living quarters. We were engaged in November of 1981 and married in August 1982."

The office affair used to mean the boss sneaking out to dinner with his secretary. But today it's just as likely to be an advertising agency account supervisor living with the head copywriter, a pharmaceutical company executive married to a physician consultant, or two attorneys from rival firms getting engaged. I think that this is a basically healthy trend that evolved in response to the recent changes in the business world, and one that will continue as women become increasingly secure about their roles in that world.

BUT WHAT IF IT'S THE BOSS?

Developing a sexual relationship with your boss is naturally a more complicated situation than getting involved with one of your peers, or even with a man highly placed in another area of the company. The risks are greater in a boss-subordinate affair, and if the relationship falls apart, you may feel that you can no longer continue to work for him. You may not be fired, but you will probably feel the need to change jobs, even if it's just a transfer to a different division of your company. (All of this is assuming that your boss is single and available. If he's married, you're only asking for trouble in every aspect of your life, and you *definitely* don't need that kind of distraction.)

Jacqueline Byrne, district manager of AT&T's corporate advertising department in New York, had a long talk with me one day about the pros and cons of office affairs. This is what she told me as I sat with her in her office on Madison Avenue. "There is nothing wrong with sex in the workplace if both of you are single. If the man happens to be your boss, there is a serious gamble involved. You may be endangering your career, and his, too, because that kind of relationship stimulates gossip and causes all kinds of complications in both your lives. But when I said that it was a gamble, that doesn't mean you have to lose. You can win." Her advice: "If you are about to enter a sexual relationship with one of your co-workers, go into it with your eyes open. Realize what you're getting yourself into. A fling is dangerous, but if there are deep mutual feelings involved, it could be a beautiful and an exciting experience. If the relationship falls apart, on your part or his or by mutual agreement, you may find it necessary to quit your job, but that's the chance you have to take. Be well aware of the risks you are taking, and *don't* take them if you're not strong enough and mature enough to endure all possible outcomes." Think of the opening song in Mel Brooks's movie, *The Twelve Chairs:* "Hope for the Best; Expect the worst."

SEXUAL HARASSMENT

This is an unpleasant subject, and something I sincerely hope you will never experience. Nonetheless, you should know that sexual harassment exists, that there are ways to protect yourself against it, and that your company has a obligation under the law to preserve your right to do your job in an environment that is free of it.

WHAT IS SEXUAL HARASSMENT?

Most experts agree that, like rape, sexual harassment has more to do with power than with sex. The comparatively recent influx of competent women into the workforce has posed a threat to some men, who feel the need to use their Y chromosome as a weapon whenever they feel that their turf is in danger.

A classic example of sexual harassment is making a woman's sexual favors the price of a job, a promotion, a raise, or an important sale or account. And the more highly placed in an organization the harasser is, the more potent the coercive effect. It is important to note here that although the vast majority of sexual harassment cases involve men using their power in an organization over women in subordinate positions, about 10 percent of cases involve women harassing men or gays hitting on straight employees. But whatever the circumstances, this kind of coercion is clearly illegal.

Where the sexual harassment laws enter a gray area is in determining which behavior in the words of the 1986 United States Supreme Court decision, "has the purpose or effect of creating an intimidating, hostile, or offensive working environment." This can cover anything from a *Playboy* calendar in the mail room to a customer's offensive jokes to a constant barrage of come-ons and lewd remarks from the men in the office.

Obviously, if your boss or a male colleague locks you in his office and lays unwelcome hands on you, you've got a serious problem that could require legal intervention. But, confronted with an occasional joke that you consider inappropriate in a business setting, or an enthusiastic "Don't *you* look nice today," it would be unwise of you to cry sexual harassment and initiate legal proceedings. Your goal is to earn respect as a professional woman, and professional women don't walk around waiting for people to knock antisexist chips off their shoulders. They have better things to do.

As I've already mentioned, I interviewed many successful women as part of my research in preparing this book, and their experiences with and reactions to sexual harassment were varied.

PROVOCATIONS—AND RESPONSES—VARY

Of all the women I spoke with in my research, only one had had an experience that was sufficiently serious for her to take action. Joan Wechsler, a former middle management executive at the ABC television network, told me that a number of years ago a male colleague of hers actually did lock her in his office one day.

"It was too horrible for me to give you the details of what happened," she said to me, "but take my word for it, it was bad. This guy should never have been permitted to work at ABC. It was just a question of time before they caught up with him, and I guess that it was his experience with me that finally did him in. He was the three-martini-lunch type, who, when he returned to his office at three or three thirty in the afternoon, would either lock his door and go to sleep or make vulgar passes at any woman who was unfortunate enough to be close to him at the moment. On this particular day, I was his target, and I was really furious over what he tried to do to me.

"I thought it over for a few days and then decided to lodge a complaint with my boss, Fred Pierce. Fred was very upset about my experience, and he assured me that he would do something about it right away. To his credit, he did. A few days later I was called in to a meeting with Fred, Elton Rule, and Leonard Goldman, his bosses. They asked me to repeat my story. I did. Then they asked me if I would be willing to testify against the man in court. I said that I certainly would. The next day the man was moved off our floor, and I never saw him again.

"I was told that a few months later he left the company. It was all handled very discreetly and quietly. I've never heard the man's name mentioned since that day. I have no idea what ever happened to him, and I really don't care. Men like that shouldn't be allowed to work in the business community."

In contrast to Joan's experience, most of the women I interviewed for this book either never had a serious, distressing, unsolicited sexual experience in their business lives or had had an occasional unpleasant encounter that, according to them, was not sufficiently important to even think about again.

I don't mean to imply that serious problems do not exist. Debbie Myers from the Interdevelopment Bank in Washington said, "I guess I've been lucky. I have been in the business world for some five years, and I have had only one bad experience with sexual harassment. In light of what I am told other women have gone through, my experience was not very important. I was working in the Minority Development Agency at the Department of Commerce in Washington. One day the man who was working in the office next to mine walked into my office and, without an introductory remark, put his arms around me and tried to kiss me. I pushed him away and hurried down the hall, distancing myself from him as quickly as possible.

"The next day, I asked my boss if he minded if I changed my office to another one a few hundred feet away, which happened to be empty at the time. He didn't ask me why, and I didn't tell him. I never made an issue out of it. I thought for a moment about lodging a complaint against the guy, but then it would have been my word against his. I never saw the man again and I promptly forgot about the incident. In fact, I don't recall ever having thought about it again until you asked the question."

Jackie Byrne reported that she had had only one unpleasant experience in all the years she worked at AT&T. "Fortunately," she told me, "it was a verbal assault rather than a physical one. The man kept coming at me with blatant suggestions, innuendos, even propositions. At first I just chose to ignore him, but that didn't work. He must have thought he could wear me down, or that I would eventually feel flattered by all the attention he was giving me. He was persistent, so I began to joke about his proposals. That didn't work either. Finally, I got angry. I confronted him one day, told him I wasn't interested, and that he should let me alone. That got through, and I was never annoyed by him again."

YOUR OWN CONDUCT IS YOUR BEST DEFENSE

Stephanie French of the Philip Morris Company commented to me, "I've never experienced sexual harrassment, and it may be because I learned a lot about dealing with men in business when I went to Harvard Business School in 1976. About seventeen percent of my class was

female, and there were unwritten social rules that were
followed by everyone. We were there to establish ourselves as serious businesswomen. In fact, I never dated my
[future] husband until a week before classes were over.
The experience at Harvard taught me certain modes of
behavior, which may be the reason I have had no problems
in my relationships with men since I became a working
woman.

"Out-of-town trips are the times when problems can
easily arise. A woman does or doesn't send out signals that
she is up for grabs. You don't hang out in the bar or have
that nightcap that is usually suggested. I go right up to my
room after dinner and finish the work that has accumulated during the day. A woman makes it clear by her
attitude what does and doesn't interest her. It doesn't have
to be spelled out in words."

Another friend of mine, associated in an important capacity for nine years with a Fortune 500 company, told me
that she has never had a sexual harrassment problem. She
believes that the reason for it has been her personal conduct. "I behave in a manner that is natural for me," she
told me. "I have always avoided situations where men
were drinking too much, and if I ever sensed a pass coming
on, I managed to get out of the situation gracefully so that
I didn't make an enemy. I also learned something a number of years ago that has held me in good stead. Whenever
I'm on a trip with a number of male associates, and the
telephone rings when I'm back in my room, I don't answer
it. I don't want to know who is calling. If I did, it would
result in an embarrassing confrontation the morning
after."

Natalia Salaczynskyj is an investment banker in New
York. When I asked her whether she had ever experienced
sexual harassment in the hallowed halls of investment

banking, she laughed. "Now that I'm with a small firm I don't experience it any longer, but when I worked with the big houses it was rampant. It was so blatant and happened so regularly that it got to a point where I wasn't even angry. I just dismissed it as a way of life and laughed it off.

"I must admit that it was rarely physical—no touching, but a consistent verbal assault. I learned to handle different approaches with different responses To one person I would say, 'Oh, get off it,' or 'Don't be silly,' or some similar nonconfrontational remark. To another more aggressive type, my response would be stronger and more aggressive. There was never a really serious incident. But I always made certain that when I said no, I didn't provoke the man into launching a vendetta against me.

"It's very easy to develop enemies as a result of situations like this, but I learned a long time ago that building a career is tough enough without the handicap of having people undermining you because their fragile egos can't stand rejection."

WHAT TO DO IF IT HAPPENS TO YOU

On June 19, 1986, in *The Meriter Savings Bank* v. *Vinson*, the Supreme Court ruled that sexual harassment is a violation of Title VII of the Civil Rights Act of 1964. But as I advised you earlier on the issue of sexual discrimination, although the law is clearly on your side if you have been subjected to sexual harassment, a lawsuit is neither the best solution to your immediate problem, nor will it figure positively in your long-term career strategy. You will be regarded much more highly if you are able to handle tough situations like these diplomatically and effectively.

If a conversation with a male colleague or client takes a turn toward the personal, it is your responsibility to steer it back to a more neutral tack. If the man makes an obvious pass, a firm but tactful "Thanks, but no thanks" may be enough to stop him. Remember that most men are neither sex-obsessed monsters nor power-blind pigs. But they are human, and if they are attracted to you, they may feel that they have nothing to lose by extending a simple invitation for drinks or dinner. If their overtures are unwelcome, it falls to you to defuse the situation in a way that they get the message but leave with their psyches intact. Your best defense is a professional demeanor that does not invite even the possibility of unwelcome advances.

A forceful physical attack is another matter entirely, however. Get away from the man as quickly as you can, however you can. To document the incident, write an account of exactly what happened, where, and when for your personal file. The man may never bother you again, but if he does, you'll find this memo a useful thing to have in your possession. Also tell a trusted female friend, preferably one who works with you, about the incident. You may find that you are not this man's first victim, and two or more of you may feel more comfortable and confident handling this situation as a united front. (You will also have a stronger case against the harasser.)

Experts advise two further counteractions at this point. First, if you can, confront the man, tell him that you want him to stop bothering you immediately, and that if he does not stop, you will be forced to report his actions to company management. Alternatively, write him a certified letter, of which you keep a copy at home, that sets down all the details regarding who, what, when, and where, and conclude by telling him to knock it off—or else. Either of these two actions will stop all but the most hardened harassers in their tracks.

If he still doesn't get the message—and at this point, you're no longer dealing with a watercooler Romeo: you've got a sick man on your hands—go to your boss and report the incident. If your boss is the harasser, go to *his* boss. Your company is legally obligated to take action on your behalf, and if you are unable to stop the harassment on the strength of your own resources, do not hesitate to bring corporate muscle to bear. As you've seen in the case of Joan Wechsler, once the facts are known, justice tends to be swift and sure.

Redken Laboratories president Paula Meehan says, "When it comes to sexual harassment, I have no sympathy or understanding. Whenever this kind of incident has been confirmed in our company, I see to it that the harasser is fired. This behavior has no place in business."

Marcia Israel, president of Judy's, a ninety-four-store chain of women's and men's sportswear shops, reacts similarly. "I've had very few cases called to my attention during all my years in business," she says, "but on those rare occasions when it has come up, I have acted swiftly. Once I confirm that sexual harassment has taken place, the man is fired immediately."

Sexual harassment, even under the Supreme Court's current definition, is an ambiguous subject, emotionally charged and highly subjective. When is a friendly smile a leer? When does a relaxed collegial relationship suddenly cross the line and become uncomfortably personal? As you've seen in the cases of Stephanie French and Natalia Salaczynskyj, your own behavior may be modified to discourage overly personal conversations or remarks, and it makes sense for you to cultivate a cordial but detached business manner. You should also not expect to uncover a potential rapist behind every file cabinet, so don't become completely unnerved if one of your male colleagues tells a joke in questionable taste every now and then. You'll know when you're on the business end of a sexual threat, and *then* you should jump in and halt the situation by whatever means are available to you.

ROGERS' RULES FOR COMBATING SEXUAL HARASSMENT

1. Don't ignore it.
2. Make it plain from the very beginning that this kind of behavior is not welcome.
3. Develop a repertoire of light but firm put-downs to try to keep an otherwise good business relationship intact.
4. If those lines don't work, look your harasser in the eye and tell him exactly how you feel. Try these responses:

- I don't appreciate your sexual remarks. In fact, I resent them.
- Please stop making remarks like that. I don't like it.
- Keep your hands off me. Our relationship is strictly a business one.
- I would hate to have to tell your boss what you're doing, but if this continues, I will.

Keep speaking to him in this manner, firmly and directly. If just telling him doesn't work, you'll have to resort to stronger measures.

5. Tell a trusted female colleague what has happened. Maybe she or someone else has been victimized but was afraid to do anything about it. Together, you can stop this.
6. Write a certified letter to your harasser at his office

or home address, spelling out in detail his insulting behavior and telling him to stop it. Keep a copy at home. (It may be useful if the situation continues.)

7. If letters and verbal protests don't stop the man, tell your boss. He or she is obligated by law to take disciplinary action against the offender.

8. If your boss is the harasser, and nothing else has stopped him, go to *his* boss. This may cost you your job, but it is much more likely that he will be fired or disciplined.

8

Mr. Right, the Biological Clock, and Other Distractions

Many young women well on their way to successful careers suddenly begin to feel that they want more from life than the best bottom line east or west of the Mississippi. Most people think of marrying at some point; however, they tend to marry later in life these days. Marrying in your thirties gives you a good ten years in which to concentrate on becoming established in the business world, but it may also increase the pressure that some women feel to have a baby.

Just as there were hundreds of choices facing you when you decided to launch a career in business, you have many, many alternatives when it comes down to life-style decisions. You could join the growing ranks of childless two-career couples and continue to channel your energy into career success, with the added advantage of having someone to talk it all over with when you finally come home from the office. You could temporarily put your own career advancement on hold and work to make your new husband more successful as he earns a degree in law, business, or medicine. Or he might support you while you acquire those extra credentials. You could drop out of the work force altogether and attend to the twenty-four-hour-a-day job of maintaining a home and raising a family. Or you may decide that you "want it all," and opt for a successful career, a husband, *and* children.

It's your choice, and it all depends on what you really want, and on the kinds of pressures you are willing to have imposed on your life. And there will be increased pressures. Adding just a husband to the equation of your daily life *squares* the complexities you have to field, rather than just doubling them. And when you figure in a child or two *and* your evolving career, you're dealing with a powder keg of pressures. Some women can handle it, but some can't.

Dr. Philippa Kennealy, currently finishing a residency at Santa Monica Hospital, said to me one day, "I am angry at the thought that, even though I want children, I fear that they will prove to be a burden. I realize it, and I accept it, but it will be interesting to see how I'll react when my career has to take a back seat during the early years when I am raising my children. My own family has always been very important to me, and I want to provide the same kind of happy homelife for my children. But I'm really not sure how I'm going to handle the career conflict problem when it arises."

Statistics indicate that most successful career women prefer to avoid the conflict altogether. Of 300 women executives polled recently by the UCLA Graduate School of Management and Korn-Ferry International, 52 percent were unmarried (never married, divorced, or widowed), and 61 percent had no children. In contrast, among male executives, only 5 percent were unmarried, and only 3 percent had no children. There are, of course, two ways of looking at this survey. You could say, "Oh my God, does that mean I can't get married, and can never have children?" Or you could say, "Great! I'll be part of the 48 percent who *will* get married, and one of the 39 percent who *will* have children."

The women I talked to while I was researching this book represented a broad range of career-marriage-family alternatives, each of which worked well for a particular woman in her particular situation. Maybe you'll be able to pick up some useful tips from their varied experiences.

RETHINKING YOUR PRIORITIES

I discussed the subject of careers with a reporter for a major paper. She told me one day about her forthcoming marriage and subsequent career plans. "I'm not as dedicated to long-range career advancement as many women are. I'm engaged to be married, and right now my fiancé and my job are 'equal partners.' I'll be married in June, and I've already bought my wedding gown. It's going to be a traditional wedding with six bridesmaids and all the trimmings.

"I'll probably work part time for a number of years, and then maybe in five years I'll think about having children. My sisters are housewives. They never liked working, but they're very happy with their domestic lives. I don't believe I would ever give up working entirely, but I do know that once I get married I won't be working from ten A.M. until eight every night, as I do now."

Carla Schalman Friedman is an account executive at Rogers & Cowan in Los Angeles. Carla's life changed dramatically when she married Sandy Friedman, another executive at our firm. "We talked about having a baby very early on," Carla explained. "Originally Sandy wasn't very enthusiastic about it, because he'd already started a family in his first marriage. But when he realized that I wouldn't regard my life as complete until I had a child, he agreed.

"When I became pregnant I knew that my life would never be the same. My priorities would change, and I knew that my child would always have to get the major share of my attention. At first the prospect of trying to juggle a job, a husband, and a child was scary. There was a time when I thought about not working, but I quickly put that thought out of my mind. I am certain now that I want to have it all, and I'm confident that I can do it.

"Working will never be the same for me again, either, because I will not be spending the same number of hours at my job as I did before. Once I learned the business and was given clients of my own to represent, it was customary for me to work twelve-hour days, from seven to seven, and I also devoted a lot of evenings and weekends to my job. I can't be that way anymore, because I want Seth to always know who his mother is.

"The baby is now my first priority, and my job will have to take second position. I'm fortunate that I work for an understanding and supportive management. They know as well as I do that the telephone calls I used to make from the office at eight in the morning or seven thirty at night can just as easily be made from home."

Attorney Rita Hauser sums it up succinctly. "You can have a husband, and you can have children, but you must decide whether the added burden is worth the price you have to pay. You may at some point decide that a husband and children are more important than your career, and if you do, don't apologize for your decision."

TWO-CAREER COMMUTERS

Kathie Berlin is a partner in the New York–based television production firm Thomas, Hart & Berlin. She is married to Richard Valeriani, the NBC news correspondent, and she has a teenage daughter, Kim, from a previous marriage. Several years ago, Kathie and her husband had an important decision to make. NBC had asked Valeriani to move to Washington. "This was an offer that would have been difficult for him to turn down," Kathie said, "because it gave him the opportunity to work with the colorful, controversial Henry Kissinger on a daily basis. At that time, I had a wonderful position with Rogers and Cowan in New York. What to do?

"We decided to have a commuter marriage. We would buy a home in Washington and keep our apartment in New York, and Kim and I would commute to Washington every weekend. Richard and I made a pact with each other, and we stuck with it for the six years that the commuting continued. We never spent a weekend apart. Neither of us was ever too tired to take the Eastern shuttle to or from Washington. Kim and I generally flew down every Friday afternoon, and we'd return to New York early Sunday evening.

"One important thing I learned was that, in order to keep sane and happy in a commuter marriage with a little child, I needed an outside support system. I just couldn't do it all myself. Fortunately, we could afford to have a maid who took care of Kim and our apartment. I call that our paid support system, but a woman in this kind of situation also needs an unpaid support system. The unpaid support system consists of family and/or friends. I don't have a New York–based family, so I struck a two-way deal with a number of friends. 'You take care of my kid once in a while,' I would say, 'and in return I'll take care of yours.' It worked. When I needed an evening for myself, that arrangement with a number of friends worked very well for me."

Kathie was able to make a commuter marriage work because, in addition to her own dedication and drive, she had the two important requirements: a supportive husband who realized the importance of her career, and the ability to get extra help when she realized that she needed it.

WHAT IT TAKES TO HAVE IT ALL

Andrea Van de Kamp was director of public affairs in the corporate offices of Carter, Hawley, Hale in Los Angeles until she became president of Independent Colleges of Southern California. She is married to John Van de Kamp, attorney general of the state of California, and they recently had a baby girl. Andrea talked with me one day about what it really takes to have it all.

"Shortly after I married John we decided to have a child," she said. "For a time I thought of retiring, but then I decided to try to have it all: be John's wife, Diana's mother, and director of public affairs at Carter, Hawley, Hale, all at the same time. I looked in the mirror and evaluated my assets and liabilities, and I decided that I could handle this tough assignment. I guess I was fortunate to have been born with enormous energy and good health. I am also a well-organized person, and consequently I am able to juggle these three jobs simultaneously with apparent success.

"The real key to having it all is that John loves my being a working woman. As for my baby, I spend early mornings with her. I am in the car pool, and I take her to school and spend time with her when I come home after work."

Stephanie French is director of cultural and contributions programs at the Philip Morris Company. Her husband is a vice president at Steuben Glass. They met when they were both students at Harvard Business School, and they have a two-and-a-half-year-old child.

"The joy of having a child is indescribable," Stephanie told me. "I never knew that life could be so fulfilling. I had been so wrapped up in my career that despite the fact that my husband was eager to start a family, I kept stalling. Having a career and a husband was tough enough, I thought, and I couldn't think of taking on the added responsibility of a child as well. Well, I never had to make the decision, because I got pregnant by accident, and that was that.

"I never even dreamed of quitting my job and pampering myself at home until the child was born. I stayed on until the last. In fact, I was dressing one morning, getting ready to go to the office, when I went into labor. I remember saying to myself that morning, 'Damn, it's so inconvenient; I have some final projects to sign off on before I go to the hospital.' But nature intervened and off to the hospital I went. I was in the hospital for three days, and I received a package from the office every day. I was away from my job for seven weeks, but I never stopped working during that time.

"My job calls for me to cover events in the evening, both in New York and out of town. But it presents no problem because my husband, who loves taking care of our child, does just that when I'm not at home. He understands and supports my comings and goings. He cooks, feeds the baby, and puts her to bed. We divide the responsibilities of child care, and each of us has our own prescribed tasks to handle. I have no guilt about the way we live our lives, because the baby, my husband, and I are all happy, and that's all that matters."

Barbara Boyle is executive vice president of production at RKO Pictures, and provocative is the word for my friend Barbara. Her views on having it all: "What's the big deal? Men have always been executives, husbands, and fathers. Why shouldn't I be a vice president, a wife, and a mother? I don't regard it as anything unusual, or any great accomplishment.

"When Kevin and I moved to Los Angeles, we decided that it was time for us to have a baby. During my first pregnancy I worked for the first seven months in my job at American International and then decided to retire for a while and concentrate on being a mother. The temporary retirement lasted longer than I had originally planned, because I immediately became pregnant again. While I was confined to my home, I started to work on some free-lance legal assignments that came my way. It was only a short time before I began to work full time again, and I continued to do so until recently, when my husband, who had retired, thought that it was time for us to spend more time together. That didn't last very long, because when an interesting offer came along we agreed that I should take it. And now I'm back doing what I've managed to do successfully for many years—having a career and a husband and children.

"Kevin and I have been married for twenty-six years. Our children are now twenty-one and nineteen. I never allowed them to be brought up by a housekeeper. They always knew who their mother was, and I was always there when they needed me. Juggling three careers—mother, wife, professional—has never been a great problem for me, because I set one rule for myself right from the outset: my husband and children always come first, and thus there was never a conflict in my mind when at any particular moment I had to choose between my job and my family. I never even presented myself with a choice; Kevin and the children were always the top priority.

"I've never felt that for me to have it all has taken a superhuman effort. Once I made my decision about what was really important in my life, it was never difficult."

THE DEBUNKING OF SUPERWOMAN

Of all the questions I asked successful women during the course of my research, this issue of jobs, husbands, and children sparked the most lively debates. Madeline Stoner, assistant professor at the Graduate School of Social Work at the University of Southern California, is strongly opposed to the idea that women must continue their careers without interruption during the years when their children are growing up. "I interrupted my career to have children," she told me. "My children were two and four when I went back to graduate school, and it wasn't until 1978 that I received my doctorate from Bryn Mawr. I planned it that way.

"I had decided that, in their early years, my children needed the full-time nurturing of their mother, without the interference that comes from the pressures of an academic life. My children are now twenty-one and twenty-five, and I don't believe that my career was at all adversely affected by the years I devoted to them."

UCLA assistant professor of history Mary Yeager agrees that women should take some time away from their careers to raise their children during the early years. After a five-year academic career at an Ivy League college, Professor Yeager arrived at UCLA in 1978. Mary married John Lithgow, the actor, five years ago. She took time off from her academic activities in 1982 to give birth to her daughter Phoebe, and in 1983 her son Nathan arrived on the scene. By any account, Mary Yeager now has it all—a successful academic career, a supportive husband, and two children. But she rejects the superwoman image.

"There's no such person as Superwoman," she said during our breakfast meeting one Saturday morning. "I've heard a lot of women talk about giving a hundred percent to each of their three jobs—wife, mother, and career woman—but I don't believe it's really possible. You must sacrifice something. You must compromise. Before I married John I gave a hundred percent of myself to the academic life, teaching, doing research, and writing. But it was a lonely, isolated, unhappy existence. I was more productive in my work than I am now, but I have so much more today than I had when I was a single woman.

"I have learned, and I have passed this observation on to my friends, that a woman who wants to have children cannot expect her career to continue in an uphill direction without interruption. There must be a number of pauses and periods of lesser activity. Anyone who has a child or children can't do it all, all the time. The first five years are exhausting, but I do believe that a woman's career can resume its upward path after those first five years.

"Women should never attempt to attain everything," Mary Yeager concludes. "Women have to make a choice during those first few years of raising children. At first I was terribly frustrated, because I felt that my work, which had been my whole life, was suddenly forced to take a position of secondary importance. But now I have learned that my present decrease in productivity will soon change direction, and my work productivity will increase so that it is at least on a par with that of any man in my department."

YOUR EMPLOYER'S POINT OF VIEW

Each of these intelligent, successful women has presented valid arguments to support her views of managing the pressure trade-offs of marriage, child rearing, and career success. But if you think that you will continue to work after you have a child, you have one more person's views to consider: your employer's. What is his attitude? What are your company's policies? It depends on who your employer is.

Rogers & Cowan, for example, is a small company. We employ about a hundred people, many of them young women. It is perhaps unrealistic to compare the attitudes of a small, family-type business like ours with those of large corporations that employ thousands of women. But I believe that, in this case, small companies may have an advantage, certainly from their employees' point of view, over the Fortune 500 megaorganizations.

I was walking down the main corridor of our New York office the other day when I noticed Debbie, one of our account executives, typing a press release with intense concentration. My eye also happened to catch a glimpse of a pink blanket close to her feet. Curious, I walked into Debbie's office. There on the floor atop the pink blanket was a tiny baby, grinning, eyes sparkling, feet kicking, arms waving. I wasn't really surprised, because I knew that Debbie had recently returned from maternity leave. I bent down, and placed my index finger close to the baby's hand. She looked at it, then slowly extended her hand and grabbed my finger. I smiled at the infant. She looked at me and returned my smile.

In the meantime, Debbie had stopped typing and was looking at me apprehensively. "What do you think?" she asked hesitantly. She had no idea what my reaction would be to seeing a four-month-old infant in residence at the Rogers & Cowan offices. "I think it's fine," I replied. "If you have no one to take care of the baby, there's no reason why you shouldn't bring her to the office with you." Debbie gave me a smile much broader than her daughter's, and although I didn't hear one, I imagine she heaved a sigh of relief. Later that same day Debbie left to meet with a client. When I walked by her office again, her secretary was feeding the baby with a bottle.

Is that good for our business? I'm sure it is. But I may not be representative of the average employer. So if you are considering having a child in the near future, and you plan to go back to work after a short leave, you should investigate your company's policies on maternity leave, flexible hours, child care, and so on. Although some organizations have not kept in step with the changing composition of the work force and its different needs, there are many companies that have made enormous strides in understanding and attempting to solve the new problems that growing numbers of working women are now facing.

Merck & Co., a large pharmaceutical company in New Jersey, recently established "flextime," a program that allows its employees to set their own working hours within certain acceptable ranges. The company has also provided on-site day care for employees' children. Merck's director of human resources says, "It is good business to be interested in an employee's welfare. If you help take away some of the stresses associated with family life, then when an employee comes to work, he or she will be able to put that much more attention to work."

The situation is improving on a nationwide basis for women who wish to have children and continue with their careers. If your company will not allow you the degree of flexibility that you, as a working mother, may require, you might want to consider seeking employment at a company whose policies offer a more liberal range of options to employees with families.

DECISIONS, DECISIONS . . .

You have some big decisions to make. Good luck.

I have tried to present both sides, *all* sides of having it all. Think carefully before you opt for it; it may be the single most important issue you will ever have to resolve for yourself.

Do you really want it all? You can have it, if you are intelligent enough, if you are willing to work hard enough, if you understand the problems to be faced, the obstacles to be overcome, and the pressures to be handled—somehow. The key is to assess your strengths realistically, to accept your limitations, and to be smart enough to call for help when you need it—and you will.

ROGERS' RULES FOR DECIDING WHETHER TO HAVE IT ALL

Ask yourself these questions:

1. Is your career success important enough to you to make all the sacrifices required worthwhile?
2. Can you handle pressure? Be honest, because having it all is synonymous with pressure, from every direction.
3. Is your husband supportive? Don't just accept lip service from him regarding sharing child care and household responsibilities; make sure that he's leveling with you. This is too important a decision to be based on wishful thinking on your part.
4. Can you afford to have someone take care of your

baby while you're at work? Can your family or your employer help you out with day care, flexible hours, and other needs?

5. If your present job really won't permit any additional distractions, is there an alternative company that you can turn to, or an alternative direction that you can take in your career?

6. Do you frequently get the guilts? If you do, forget about juggling a job, a husband, and children. You'll always feel that one of them is not receiving enough of your attention.

7. Realize that this is the most important personal and professional decision you may ever make, and ask yourself the question a thousand times, and think and rethink your answer a thousand times: Do I really want to have it all? A career? A husband? Children???

9

Women Entrepreneurs: Heading for the Top Without the Corporate Ladder

So far, every career strategy I've outlined, every guideline and tip I've brought to your attention, has been directed at the young woman working her way up the corporate ladder. But it's important for you to know that there are *other* ladders, and that an increasing number of women are climbing them successfully. Starting and running your own business is the ultimate challenge in today's business environment, and many ambitious women, who may feel out of place in the old boys club atmosphere of a major corporation, are choosing the independent and potentially rewarding path of the entrepreneur.

WHAT MAKES AN ENTREPRENEUR?

At some point you will ask yourself, "What do I really want to do with my life?" You may have dealt with that awesome query before you began to look for your first job, or it may have occurred to you a year, two years, or five years after you launched your career. Answering the question will require an honest assessment of those career and life-style variables that are most likely to lead you to achieve your goals for personal and financial satisfaction.

If you are disappointed with the progress you have been making toward those goals, if you are beginning to feel that your present career track will never bring you the money or the freedom you'll need to achieve the life-style you want, and if the corporate life, with its office politics, its military hierarchy, its unpredictable changes of direction, and its day to day frustrations and anxieties, is beginning to make you wonder whether it's all worthwhile, you may be tempted to think about going into business for yourself, about becoming an entrepreneur.

Dr. Richard Buskirk, Director of the entrepreneur program at the University of Southern California School of Business Administration, describes an entrepreneur as "someone who undertakes an economic venture with the hope of somehow making some money from it. It is a person who has control over his or her own destiny."

A number of times in this book I have quoted my good friend Barbara Corday, who, as president of Columbia Pictures Television, was one of the most important executives in the entertainment industry. While I was writing this chapter, Barbara received a telephone call from New York. She was told that she was fired, and she was out of her office the next morning. She was caught in the corporate crossfire between Columbia Pictures, the Coca-Cola Company, and Tri-Star Pictures. The new boss wanted someone else in her job. No one ever gave her any more explanation than that, and she was out with one telephone call. That can never happen to you if you are an entrepreneur.

I know a bit about entrepreneuring because I have been doing it all my professional life. With the exception of one six-month period when I was twenty, and worked as an office boy in a Hollywood publicity office, I have never had a job. I have always been in business for myself. Never having had a job was neither an accomplishment nor a disgrace. For me it was simply a necessity brought about by a stroke of fate. I had been going to secretarial school in Los Angeles after having completed three years of college, because I was told by friends that movie producers were hiring male secretaries, and the thought of working in a motion picture studio intrigued me. But fate diverted me from what was then my goal when one day I dropped by my sister Estelle's office to drive her back to our parents' home, where we both lived. Estelle was working as a secretary in a Hollywood publicity office. She introduced me to her boss. Her boss told me that she needed an office boy. Did I want the job?

Of course I did. It meant that I would no longer be a financial drain on my family, I could support myself. The next day I quit secretarial school and my initiation into the publicity business began. My boss was Grace Nolan, a woman who owned her own business. (Yes, there were women entrepreneurs back then.) My job lasted six months. I did something stupid one day, Mrs. Nolan literally blew her stack, and I was back on the street looking for a job.

Those were the days of the Great Depression, the 1930s. Men were selling apples on the street for a nickel, the unemployment lines were never-ending, and it came as no surprise to me that no one had a job for a twenty-one-year-old whose only job experience was a six-month stint as an office boy. I liked the publicity business, the little of it I'd seen. If Grace Nolan could earn a living at it, I could too, I reasoned. I persuaded my financially strapped father to lend me five hundred dollars, and with that capital, Henry C. Rogers Publicity opened for business a few weeks later in a one-room office on Hollywood Boulevard.

I have owned my own business ever since. There have been good times and bad times. It took me about five years before I was able to say to myself, "Yes, I think I'm going to make it." There were a hundred days, maybe even a thousand, that were filled with despair, but I never considered giving up. Even when I had learned enough about publicity that there was a chance I could get a "real" job, the thought never occurred to me. I had been fired once, and I didn't like it; I would never put myself in a position where I could be fired again.

WHAT IT TAKES TO BE AN ENTREPRENEUR

I know many women entrepreneurs. They run big businesses and small businesses. Marcia Israel is the founder and CEO of Judy's, a large chain of retail clothing stores. Paula Meehan is founder and CEO of Redken Hair Products. And Mary Wells started the New York advertising agency Wells Rich Green. There are also a number of talented women who launched their careers working at Rogers & Cowan and left to set up their own public relations businesses. These women all have a number of traits in common.

•*They are fully committed.* They don't think of their work as a nine-to-five commitment, nor do they take two-hour lunches unrelated to work. They are dedicated to their businesses, dedicated to success.

•They had the courage to take the plunge. When the moment of truth arrived and they had to decide whether to stay in their present positions, move on to other jobs, or take the risk of going into their own businesses, each of them said, "I'm ready to go for it."

•They have boundless energy and initiative. I guess that every successful woman has energy and initiative, but the entrepreneur must have these two character traits in abundance even *before* she arrives at the decision to strike out on her own. The entrepreneur sets her own pace, and if she is destined for success, that pace is a fast one. She doesn't think about the hours. No one is telling her what to do. She makes up her own rules and her own work habits as she goes along, and those self-imposed rules are always more stringent and more demanding than any rules handed down by someone else.

•They are problem-solvers. Not everyone knows how to get things done, and not everyone has sufficient common sense and mental flexibility to solve problems. Think for just a moment about the fact that many people working in a corporate environment never have to worry about getting things done and solving problems. Corporate jobs have job descriptions, job rules, job procedures. Everything is spelled out. Routine problems have already been solved by others, so the average employee just has to place herself on the assembly line every morning and follow the route that others have taken a thousand times before. But not the entrepreneur. She seeks out new solutions every

day, she discovers new ways to get things done, she improvises.

A PSYCHOLOGICAL SNAPSHOT OF THE SUCCESSFUL ENTREPRENEUR

The successful entrepreneur invariably is the person who puts forth the added effort. She has tremendous intensity and dedication and is always willing to make that last telephone call, try that one last time, stay at the office that extra hour in the evening. It's really that let's-try-it-once-more attitude that spells the difference between success and failure.

Like the successful corporate executive, the successful entrepreneur has the ability to sell herself. She can persuade people to do many things: to lend her money, to work hard for her, to buy from her—in short, to do what she wants them to do.

She is motivated by the need to prove something to someone. This person may be a parent or a former teacher, or an ex-husband who thought she'd never amount to anything. Sometimes she simply has the need to prove something to herself.

Many entrepreneurs also have the need to compensate for some inadequacy or to atone for a previous failure. I have been told, although I have never been conscious of it, that my success stems from the fact that I stuttered very badly when I was a child. One reason that I seek out speaking engagements now, experts say, is that I am still proving to myself that I have overcome my stuttering problem.

Entrepreneurs are dissatisfied with the status quo, even if it's success. They want to pile other successes on top of the present one they should be enjoying. I first noticed this trait in myself when it became apparent that I was getting little satisfaction out of my mid-life success. I then learned that the climb to the top of the mountain is much more gratifying than the view from the top. The solution: get down and look for another mountain to climb.

The successful entrepreneur is convinced that she's the only one who can make it happen. President Harry S. Truman is said to have originated the phrase "The buck stops here." An entrepreneur truly has no one to pass the buck to. She takes full responsibility for the success of her business.

WHAT IT DOESN'T TAKE TO BE AN ENTREPRENEUR

•*A résumé as long as your arm.* You don't need twenty years of work experience before you go into business for yourself. If most successful entrepreneurs waited until they'd gained sufficient experience before they got started, they'd never have started. I'm not implying that business knowledge and experience are unimportant, but they may not be the most important factors in determining your success. When women entrepreneurs gather together at meetings or conventions, they invariably talk about Lore Harp, a housewife who founded Vector Graphics in 1976 and built a twenty-five-million-dollar computer manufacturing concern—though in the beginning she didn't know anything about computers: Those who have observed her success sometimes conjecture that if she had first gained some experience at IBM, Digital, or Wang, she might have built a fifty-million-dollar or one-hundred-million-dollar business. But it's equally valid, to argue that if she'd started at IBM, she might never have had the incentive or the nerve to go into her own business.

Of course, if you are embarking on the kind of business venture that requires financing over and beyond what you can supply yourself, a certain degree of experience is a plus. It is unlikely that a prospective investor will back you unless you have some kind of successful track record. In this situation, you really have to back up what you *say* you can do, and your ability to persuade investors to finance you frequently depends on what you've done so far.

•*A big idea.* Venture capitalists have would-be entrepreneurs pounding on their doors every day with "big ideas." But it's a long road from a big idea to a big business, or even a successful small one. A lot of people who have a trunk full of big ideas rarely if ever are able to turn those ideas into profitable operations. Usually these big-idea people are so in love with those ideas that they are unable to analyze them and see their weak points.

The fact is that you don't need a big idea to go into business. All you need is an ordinary idea for a product or service that can generate income. Does home-cooked food sound like a big idea? People have been selling food out of their homes for hundreds, maybe thousands of years, yet Sarabeth Levine started selling her homemade apricot-orange marmalade to Bloomingdale's in New York in 1981, and she's now running a four-million-dollar-a-year business.

Three years ago, Nancy Atkins Keresty parlayed her ability to knit into a start-up knitwear business. Using $20,000 of her savings as seed capital, she lost $8,000 the first year, showed a $15,000 profit the second year, and is now on her way to building a substantial enterprise.

Just a few years ago, Anna Sellibello started to make

decorative tiles in the basement of her New Jersey home. Now her Dover, New Jersey company sells fifteen lines of decorative tiles to a hundred national tile distributors.

I won't bore you with the mighty-oaks-from-little-acorns theme, but these three women and many, many others prove that you don't need a big idea to build a successful business.

•A pot of gold. It doesn't have to take a lot of money to become an entrepreneur. Sometimes when I interview a talented person for whom I have no immediate job opening at Rogers & Cowan, I ask them, "Have you ever thought about getting into the public relations business for yourself?" In most cases, the answer comes back, "Oh, I couldn't do that. I don't have the money it would take." I then reply, "But you can do it without money," and I explain how it can be done.

To start up in the public relations business, and in many other service or consulting businesses, all you need is a desk and a typewriter (or a personal computer). You can easily get away, at the outset at least, without an office and without a secretary. No one ever said, of course, that starting a business was easy. And there's no question that if you have money available to you, many problems are less pressing than if you don't have access to a solid wad of capital. But the point is, if the money just isn't there, you'll have to figure out how you can get what you need without it—if becoming an entrepreneur is something you really want.

When you are starting out on your own without capital, think in terms of going into the kind of business that requires only minimal financial investment. One alternative is to take over someone else's business. Look around. Talk to people. Earlier in this book I discussed networking, and this is another situation in which networking is required. Who has a business that he or she is trying to get out of or is willing to sell at a bargain-basement price? There are a lot of reasons why people who own a business would want to get rid of it, but the most likely reason is that the business is unsuccessful because it has been badly managed. You can find yourself taking over that business and owning a substantial percentage of it if you can convince the present owners that you are the person who can turn the business around by managing it properly and giving them an opportunity to recoup their losses.

Finally, if you realize that a certain amount of capital is required for the particular venture that interests you, try to get that money from other people. As a member of the advisory board of the entrepreneur program at the University of Southern California, I often meet with the program director, Dr. Richard Buskirk. One day he and I were lunching at the faculty club, and I asked him how his students handle start-up finance problems once they've graduated from school and begun their careers as entrepreneurs. "We teach them," he replied, "that the ideal business requires you to invest no money. No investment, no loss. The basic managerial philosophy of the modern entrepreneur is to furnish the skill for a venture and let other people put up the money." He tells his students, "Let others take the financial risk. You risk your time, effort, and reputation."

Your success in raising capital will be directly proportional to your business credibility. Even if you first approach your parents, relatives, or friends, it's your responsibility to convince them that you have the skills required to run a successful business. Don't expect them to lend you the money or invest in your plan because of who you are. You will derive greater satisfaction from starting a business if you know that your investors were won over by your credibility, your sincerity, your intelligence and abilities, rather than because you are someone's daughter, niece, or friend.

• *Wild-card risks.* You might think that becoming an entrepreneur presents you with incalculable risks. It just isn't so. It's been said a thousand times by business executives, business school professors, bankers, and economists: business isn't risky—people are. If you plan your business wisely and carefully, your risk of failure is minimized. But *you* are the main risk factor; if you're inept, if you're lazy, if you're not alert to the signs of change in the market, you won't make it. Sixty-five percent of new businesses in this country don't. If you really have what it takes, going into business for yourself is no more risky than working for someone else—and waiting for the axe to fall.

IT'S NEVER TOO EARLY TO START

Don't make the mistake of thinking that you must work at at job for five or ten years before you strike out on your own. It's been said that many people who work for ten years do not have ten years of experience. They have one month of experience repeated 120 times.

When Joanne McClure was a student in the entrepreneur's program at USC, she developed a glass-etching process that proved to be an interesting new way to display diplomas, awards, and citations. She knew that she had the potential to build a substantial business, so she convinced members of the USC faculty to take her on after graduation at a decent full-time secretary's salary. In one year she had saved enough money to start her business and support herself with no additional income for six months. And today Joanne is running her own very successful business.

As of this writing, Betsy Ross is still a business school student, and she has already launched her entrepreneurial career. She buys water-repellent disposable surgical scrub suits from a hospital supply house. Then she paints them, redesigning them as Halloween costumes and as Raiders, Rams, Lakers, Trojans, or Bruins uniforms, and sells them at college or professional sports events.

Age and experience can be very useful in business, and there is much to know and much to learn in every industry, but there are times when it's advantageous to just roll the dice and learn as you go along.

IT'S NEVER TOO LATE TO START

Starting a business may not seem like a viable option— or even an attractive one—at this early stage in your career, but you should keep in mind that there are many routes to the top. Even if you opt for the corporate life now, there's no reason why you couldn't start your own business five, ten, or twenty years from now.

Daniella Kuper, an owner of the Kuper-Finlon advertising agency, never dreamed of running her own business. It wasn't until she married, had two children, and had her marriage fall apart that she decided to launch a career in business. And instead of looking for any old job, she became an entrepreneur.

Francesca Lack runs a profitable public relations business in New York. Her offices are in one of those new high-rise buildings in the high-rent district, and she has a staff of fifteen assisting her. Francesca recently described to me how she got started six years ago. "I decided that

I didn't want to work from home, that I would have a greater incentive to build a successful business if I had an office to go to every morning. I walked up and down Fifth, Madison, and Park avenues and stopped in every office building. I looked for the manager of the building and asked whether any of the tenants had extra space that they would be willing to sublet. At long last I found two little available furnished offices, which I rented for three hundred dollars a month. I lugged my typewriter from home and leased another one for my secretary, who came with me from my previous position. She was willing to accept a much lower salary than she had been receiving, because she was intrigued with the prospect of being part of a start-up situation. A week later I got my first client and I was in business."

Josie Cruz Natori owns a twelve-million-dollar lingerie business. Before entering the ranks of entrepreneurs, she worked in the corporate finance departments of the Bach Group and Merrill Lynch, and she went on to become a vice president in Merrill Lynch's investment banking division. But after nine years, she began to feel stifled working for other people and having no control over her life. At the age of thirty she went into business for herself, and today her beautiful designs are sold in major department stores and fine specialty shops across the country.

ENTREPRENEURIAL STYLE

One of the wonderful freedoms that comes with entrepreneuring is that each entrepreneur can develop her own style of doing business. However, there are certain essentials that you should incorporate into your personal style.

Although you may feel a bit daunted or insecure when

you're first starting out, you must train yourself to exude confidence and enthusiasm. When they realize that you're new at this game, some people may make allowances for you—but not for long. Bankers, vendors, investors—really anyone you come in contact with in the course of doing business—are accustomed to working with professionals, and it is important for you to develop a winning professional style.

ROGERS' RULES FOR DEVELOPING ENTREPRENEURIAL STYLE

1. You must immediately create the impression that you are a serious, dedicated businesswoman. You may have just graduated from college, or you may have a husband and two children at home. It doesn't matter. The people you deal with want to know that you are serious about your business, and not just acting on a whim that you may abandon tomorrow.

2. Enthusiasm is one of the essentials in the entrepreneur's professional style. You must show great interest in and excitement about your business and make everyone aware that it is the most important thing going on in your life. Your excitement will be conveyed to the people you're talking to, and they'll get caught up in it and be much more likely to buy whatever it is you're selling.

3. Presenting a positive image of yourself is another essential. If you don't present yourself in a positive light, no one else is going to see you that way. Marilyn Pultz, a entrepreneurism career counselor, advises her clients to present themselves as individuals of competence, knowledge, and talent. Careful advance preparation for any business meeting will help you to project a positive image. Rehearse what you are

going to say, be ready with good answers to any questions you can anticipate, and concentrate on emphasizing your strengths.

4. You must develop a sensitivity to the needs and wants of others, while at the same time asserting your own needs. You must learn to listen carefully and to learn quickly from what you hear. Too many people are so busy thinking about what they are going to say that they neglect to listen to the other guy. You'll never sell him if you don't know what he thinks he needs to buy.

5. Right from the start you should let people know that you are a woman of integrity who honors her commitments. You must render the highest quality of service, do your best for your clients or customers, and quickly become recognized for your straight dealing and reliability.

6. You must be flexible, willing to adapt to change and to learn. Different problems require different kinds of solutions, and you must be able to take advantage of changes in the market as they occur. Stay informed; never let yourself be blindsided by something new that could damage your business. You should think of your business, and of the business environment as a whole, as undergoing constant metamorphosis.

Rogers' Rules for Successful Entrepreneurs

1. You must have enormous drive, energy, ambition, and persistence.

2. You must be motivated by the need to control your own destiny and to be in a position where other people can't tell you what to do or when to do it.

3. You must be willing to push yourself to the limit, sometimes beyond your comfort zone.

4. You must believe in yourself and have confidence that

you will be able to solve the problems that will inevitably arise.

5. You must accept the fact that there will be setbacks, mistakes, and failures but you must not let them discourage you. Rather, let them motivate you even more strongly to succeed.

10

Now *You're* the Boss

One day your boss will invite you to lunch, or ask you to come into his office. You've put in the hours, you've made yourself visible in the organization, you've established a great track record of solid achievements. You've performed superbly in your job, and this is the moment when you'll know it was all worthwhile. You're offered a promotion to a position with management responsibilities. Now you're in the club; you're a boss, a member of the management team. You can hardly believe it—is this what an out-of-body experience feels like? You hear yourself thanking your boss for the opportunity, promising to do your best to fulfill your new responsibilities, and setting up a meeting for the next morning to discuss the goals and priorities for your new assignment.

You float back to your desk. Then the thought, "My God! I can't do *that!*" flashes through your mind. "I don't know the first thing about managing people. What if I fail? My career would be over before it got started."

Congratulations; you've just experienced the reaction

that hits most of us when we're faced with a new challenge. But just as you learned to ride a two-wheeler when you were a little girl and learned to read French in high school or college, you can learn to become a manager, and a good one, too. This chapter will point out some strategies for managing the transition from subordinate to manager, and whether you've been managing a staff of two or two hundred for a year or more, you may still be able to gain some new insights into becoming a great boss.

Just one question before we get started: do you really want to be a boss? When you were just someone's subordinate, you were judged solely on your own accomplishments. Now you'll also be evaluated on the performance of the people who report to you. Are you comfortable with this kind of extended accountability? Your boss obviously has confidence in your leadership abilities, but being a boss requires not only that you *have* those abilities but also that you possess the desire, the will, and the driving ambition to exercise them. Part of your time will now be spent managing, and you'll have to delegate some of the hands-on work to your subordinates. Many people enjoy the "real work" aspects of their jobs, and they prefer to remain specialists in their areas of expertise rather than operating one-step-removed, as a manager. Your decision will depend upon your own definition of career success and job satisfaction, but if you've decided to accept the challenge of management responsibilities, read on!

IT'S A WHOLE NEW BALLGAME

How true it is! Even if you are now simply heading up a department in which you've been working for some time, you will be perceived as a different person by your co-workers.

Jean Firstenberg told me about her early days on the job as director of the American Film Institute. "Although I had had jobs before," she said, "this was my first experience in running an organization with some twenty-five people reporting to me. My first task was to deal with my self-image. I had to accept myself as a boss before I could expect anyone else to accept me in that position. This took some adjustment on my part, but it hit me like a ton of bricks when I woke up one day and realized that people were looking at me differently than they had the day before. They saw me as a Boss, and that realization made me aware that I was a different person than I'd been before.

"I wasn't frightened. Maybe I didn't know enough, didn't know what I was getting into, to be frightened. There was the problem of accepting the responsibility of leadership, and I still struggled with my self-image to sense myself as a leader. That was the original turmoil: to accept myself in this role."

Terrie Williams is vice president of public relations at Essence Communications, one of the largest black-owned companies in the country. I asked her to tell me about her reactions on the day that she became a boss. "It was an exhilarating but frightening experience," she replied. "I was accustomed to doing everything myself, and it was very difficult for me to delegate some of what had been my own responsibilities to others. The transition from being a subordinate to stepping into a position of authority is a difficult one, and anyone who makes that transition must realize that it doesn't happen overnight. It's a long, long pull."

Suzanne de Passe joined Motown Records in 1968 in an entry level position. In February 1981, she was named president of Motown Productions, the division responsible for all motion picture and television activity in the company. "When I first became a boss," Suzanne told me recently, "I had been named creative director of West Coast recording operations. The day of the announcement, four Motown employees wore black armbands to work in protest against my appointment. Their protests were based on the fact that I was a woman, I was young, and I had replaced a man they liked.

"I had to make a fast decision. It was them or me. The following day I fired three of them. I had quickly decided that there was no way for me to run a successful operation without the complete support of everyone in my department. They had to go, and despite the agony it caused me, it was something I had to do. I wondered what the reaction of everyone else in the company would be to what could have been perceived as a ruthless act. But there wasn't a ripple; everyone must have realized that I did what I had to do.

"For many months I apologized to everyone for being a boss. I found it difficult, because I had started at the bottom at Motown, to ascend what some people at the company referred to as 'the throne.' "

It is difficult for many women (men, too) to give up their collegial, "team" relationships with their co-workers and assume the lonelier role of leader. But as Natasha Josefowitz wisely cautions the new manager, in her book, *You're the Boss.*

If you don't revise your social behavior, you will have an impossible task when you need to refuse favors, or have to reprimand, discipline, demote, or even fire people who are friends. It does not mean that you are not a friend, but that you're a boss first. If you choose to remain "equal," you may be liked but not respected. If you choose to accept your dominant position, you may lose the pleasant camaraderie, but you will earn respect if you are a fair boss.

It is not an easy choice, but it must be made at the start. Your workers will be watching you closely to see what you do. Don't count

on their making it easy for you; it is to their advantage to keep you
at their level. There are exceptions: where group work is effective
without formal leadership, or when workers can begin their jobs on
their own and can control their own results, the supervisor may still
be accountable to higher-ups but may be more of a team member
than a leader.

You do not have to be a dictator, but you owe your
subordinates the security of knowing that someone is in
charge.

R-E-S-P-E-C-T

You must remember when you take over your first
managerial position that you have not entered a popularity
contest. You are not there to be liked. You are there to get
things done.

It is essential for you to be respected. I don't discount
the advantages of being liked, and if you are able to relate
to your subordinates in such a way that you can be both
respected and liked, you'll be one up on many other people
in your position. Never forget, though, that being respected is your top priority.

To win the respect of your subordinates, you must be
knowledgeable about your job and theirs, and capable of
communicating that knowledge to them. You must also be
firm and consistent, and you must not waffle on a decision
once you've made it. You must treat all your employees
alike, putting aside your personal feelings about them as
individuals. Your staff will be watching you closely to see
whether you have certain favorites who get special treat-
ment from you. But it's your responsibility to treat equally
those you like, those you dislike, and those you don't really
care about one way or the other. It's difficult to be that
objective, but it's important for you to give it your best
effort.

It is essential that your instructions are carried out promptly. If you allow some of your staff to ignore your policies or your instructions, or you permit them to react later than you expect them to, you will lose the respect of your subordinates, and it will be more difficult—if not impossible—to manage them successfully.

You must stay at least one step ahead of your team at all times. If you are not on top of everything, if you don't know what they're doing and they discover that you don't, they will be quick to take advantage of your weakness. This does not mean that you must know specific and detailed daily comings and goings of each member of your staff, but you must be sufficiently tuned in so that you can determine who's doing his job properly, and who isn't.

Don't be surprised if you discover that your people are testing you. Watch for the signals they send out. They want to know how good you really are, how much you know and how much you don't know. These mind games come with the territory; don't let them rattle you. Just stay alert, and never stop learning—you'll pass every test.

MANAGEMENT STYLES

There are probably as many management styles as there are managers. Nonetheless, this seemingly infinite variety of options divides fairly neatly between two management philosophies: autocratic and democratic. Autocratic managers assume that people basically don't want to work, and that they will do as little as they possibly can, short of performing so ineptly that they lose their jobs as a consequence. Autocrats hold that people must be forced to work, that they must be threatened to perform even adequately, and that they must be constantly and minutely supervised.

In contrast, let me make it clear that democratic management is not management in which workers have a one-person, one-vote role in corporate affairs. The democratic manager seeks out the advice, counsel, and point of view of her subordinates. Then, after seriously listening to what every one has to say, she makes her own decision.

Democratic managers believe that people are willing to work, and that they enjoy working up to capacity and increasing their capacity, particularly if they are motivated, encouraged, and directed, and if they receive feedback and coaching from their managers. I, of course, recommend the democratic philosophy, because I believe that it produces better results. If you decide to adopt an autocratic style, however, make certain that you are able to accurately read the moods of your staff, and don't push so hard that you find yourself with a rebellion on your hands.

Marcia Israel, founder of a chain of sportswear shops that grosses $60 million annually, tells new bosses, "You must be exemplary. To be an effective boss you must be respected, and in order to win respect you must behave in an exemplary manner. I have to resort to a children's expression, 'monkey see, monkey do,' which is a fact of life. If you put your feet on your desk, if you spend half your day with personal telephone calls, and if you take half a dozen coffee breaks during the day, you can't expect your employees to act otherwise. You will get the most out of your people by serving as a role model for them to emulate."

Louise Sunshine is a New York–based real estate entrepreneur. She talked with me one day about the way she structures relationships with her subordinates. "I try to motivate them, and they learn a lot from me. I give them nourishment, and then I sit back and let them grow. I don't feel threatened by them, and I make sure that they get involved in everything I do. Recently one of my marketing people brought me a deal, and I involved her in all the partners' meetings and negotiations that went on over a number of months. Although eventually the deal fell through, this first experience in deal making gave her the opportunity to develop her entrepreneurial talents, and gave her the satisfaction of being involved in every step of the development of a real estate deal. The next time, she will have the added satisfaction of working through a deal to its successful conclusion."

Kate Ford, vice president and creative director at the Ford Model Agency, told me about the period in her life when she first assumed management responsibilities. "In my present position, I'm the boss to a staff of some sixty people, and I've learned a lot about managing since I first started. At the beginning I tried to be everyone's best friend, but that didn't really work. I discovered that it's important to keep everyone at a certain distance in order to get things done. I'm not a screamer, and for me the soft management approach gets the best results. I deal directly with our people, keep track of everyone's performance, and give raises when I feel they are warranted. When anyone's performance falls below the acceptable level, I spend time with them, I encourage them to try harder, and I try to find out if there's anything bothering them."

Philip Morris Company executive Stephanie French has developed a democratic management style that works well for her. "I came up through the ranks and learned how to be a boss by watching the people around me. And I observed early on that different management styles were right for different people. I decided that the we're-all-in-this-together approach was the one that could work most effectively for me. I was never concerned about establishing my authority, because once I demonstrated to my associates that I knew my business I was accepted as a boss. I established a common bond with my associates. They knew early on that if problems arose we would work them out together, and that their opinions were as valid as mine."

YOUR STAFF: CARE AND FEEDING

From the moment that your new position is announced, you are responsible for the success or failure of the people who report to you. You can reward them, rebuke them, or ignore them—and they may not view your new power over them as the best thing that ever happened to their careers.

- Both men and women staff members may feel awkward or anticipate some loss of prestige working for a woman manager.
- They will wonder how much power you really have in the organization.
- They may think you've slept your way to the top.
- They may repeatedly and ingeniously challenge your authority.
- They may try to ignore you, or to work around you.

Does this make your blood boil? Try to stay cool. Your relationship with your staff is a two-way street. You can make or break their careers, and they, to a significant degree, hold the same power over you. Management is watching *you.* If your staff suddenly begins to function more productively than they had under their previous manager, you'll get the credit. If their performance falls below former standards, you'll get the blame.

You will be tested by your employees; all bosses are, in one way or another. But understand that much of their initial distrust of you may stem from their own insecurity. They were going along, doing their jobs, feeling fine—and suddenly there's a change at the top. Will you want your own team? Will you make radical changes in time-honored procedures, areas of responsibility, *turf?*

Try to view this new situation through the eyes of your staff, and try to understand and anticipate their fears and their needs in these circumstances. Do they require more attention from you now? Would they like you to come and see them in their offices, instead of always being called to yours? Are they interested in telling you about their jobs, their complaints, about their suggestions for streamlining procedures and achieving higher productivity? You bet they are. Once you put yourself in their shoes, it will be easier for you to behave in such a way that you are able to win their support.

I have discovered what may be the best solution to boss-subordinate relations. It's just the Golden Rule: Do unto your employees as you would have your boss do unto you. Think about this for a minute. It sums up in a few words everything you have to know about becoming an effective boss. Think how many times you've thought

- I wish my boss would say something nice to me.
- I wish my boss would tell me what he thinks of the job I'm doing.
- I wish my boss would pay more attention to me.
- I wish my boss would listen when I'm talking to him.
- I wish my boss wouldn't criticize me the way he does.
- I wish my boss would offer to help me improve my performance.

You can probably think of fifty more I-wish-my-boss-woulds. Write them all down. Then turn them around and see how they apply to *you* as a boss. Reread your list, substituting "I will" for "I wish my boss would." Pay attention to this list, and you will develop into the kind of manager who will continue to rise ever higher in the organization.

MOTIVATING YOUR EMPLOYEES

You will begin to be recognized as a good boss when you learn to motivate your employees to their highest level of performance. Your subordinates probably won't give you their best automatically. After all, it's easier to coast than to accelerate. But people are happier, I think, when they're doing well—and being recognized for their accomplishments. To keep your staff supercharged.

- offer them interesting and challenging assignments.
- give them immediate positive feedback on a job well done.
- make them feel important, and that you care about them as individuals and as team members.
- set goals for them, and make sure that you and they agree on their priorities.
- give them reasonable work loads, but make sure they know that you expect high-level performance from them.
- encourage creativity, innovative thinking, and fresh approaches to problem solving.

CRITICISM: HOW TO DISH IT OUT—AND HOW TO TAKE IT

Before you criticize one of your subordinates, stop and think. What is the objective of your criticism? You'll probably answer, "Well, he did it all wrong and I have to tell him," or, "She made a serious mistake, and I have to call her on the carpet for it," or even, "He just makes me so mad the way he does things."

Now take a minute and really think it through. Have you ever done anything wrong? Have you ever made a mistake? Have you ever made anyone angry because of something you did? Of course you have. Everyone has. That's no reason for *not* criticizing people; when they need to be corrected, they should be. But keep your objective firmly in mind. *The objective of criticism should be to improve a subordinate's performance the next time.*

That is the only reason ever to criticize people. Someone made a mistake. How can you help to prevent this person from making the same mistake again? Not by yelling, but by explaining calmly and fully what was done wrong, and how to do it differently if the situation occurs again.

In my recent book, *Rogers' Rules for Success,* I gave the recipe for what I call Rogers' Criticism Sandwich: the most effective way to dish out criticism, and the way that lessens the hurt and resentment the object of your criticism automatically feels, is to layer it between two slices of praise. Start with a statement of reassurance, state your criticism as constructively and as sensitively as possible, and then end the discussion with a final note of praise and respect, and a compliment. That's the way to keep your subordinates motivated and happy in their work.

But what about those times when you're on the *receiving* end of a critical remark? The person who is critical of you will most likely not be as diplomatic and as sensitive as I have suggested you be. And just as there is a right way and a wrong way to dish it out, there is a right way and a wrong way to take it. The wrong way is to get angry, defensive, and bitter. The better way, and the one that I hope you will choose, is to react unemotionally and objectively, and to evaluate carefully whether the criticism is justified or not. If the criticism is justified, thank your critic, and tell him or her that you will try to do better the next time. If you feel that he or she is out of line, listen very carefully and ask for specific examples so that you and the other person both know exactly what the alleged problem is. Arguing about criticism that is directed at you is a waste of time, and it's destructive to the boss-subordinate relationship.

HIRING

When you first stepped into your new managerial job, you probably inherited a staff that had been put together by someone else. But eventually, as a result of departures, or because the department's responsibilities have grown under your leadership, you will find yourself in the challenging and often frustrating position of having to hire one or several new employees.

Before you begin the hiring process, you must fully understand the requirements of the job for which you will be interviewing applicants. Although you may have a tendency to say, "Oh, I know what the job entails," there is a better than even chance that you don't know the job as well as you think you do. There must be a job description somewhere in the company. If you work in a large organization you will probably find the relevant job description in the personnel department. If you work for a small company you may discover that no written job description exists for this position. Solution: draft one yourself, and then, to make certain that you're on the right track, talk with a number of your peers and with your boss to get added input.

Once you have a workable job description on paper,

prepare a list of questions to ask the applicants. (A note of caution: make sure that your questions are strictly job related. Federal law prohibits you from asking questions of a personal nature—age, marital status, religious affiliation, etc.)

When it is time for you to interview the applicants, try to arrange to conduct the interviews without interruptions. Remember that each interview is as important to you as it is to the applicant, and you do a disservice to both of you if you permit constant interruptions in your conversation. Try to give each applicant your undivided attention. I would also suggest that you not sit behind your desk. I always think that a desk that separates me from the other person sets up a psychological block. It is much better to get out from behind your desk and sit in a chair opposite but fairly close to the applicant.

First impressions are dangerous. They have a tendency to prejudice you in favor of or against the person. Make notes on your first impressions, but remember that they might not be important factors when it comes time to make a final decision. Although all of us are influenced by shined or unshined shoes and clean or dirty fingernails, these are superficial details that might or might not have a bearing on the person's qualifications for the job.

Try to put people at ease. Smile, and try to establish an informal atmosphere. You might want to offer applicants coffee or a soft drink. You can mention that you understand how stressful job interviews are because you have gone through them yourself. It is to your advantage if applicants feel they can relate to you, and that you are sympathetic to their lack of ease in this situation.

Now it's time for you to ask your questions. Your objective is to get the applicants to open up and talk. Don't accept yes-or-no answers. Encourage applicants to expound on the subjects you are asking about. Explain what you are seeking to learn through the interview. Job applicants, largely inexperienced in being put on the spot like this, have a tendency to go off on tangents and stray from the subject. It's important to interrupt these conversational wanderings and get people back on track.

If you find that applicants are uncommunicative, or that they have presented themselves ineffectively, it may be your fault, not theirs. Remember that they are nervous, and possibly insecure. You're the one in control, and it is your responsibility to ask the kinds of questions that will let them feel comfortable and begin to talk freely.

If, after fifteen or twenty minutes of conversation, you decide that an applicant is a hopeless case, it is time to call a halt to the interview. Thank the person for their time, and tell them that they'll be hearing from you. If you think, however, that a person might be a serious candidate for the job, it is now time for you to describe the job and explain your performance expectations, how standards are set and evaluated, details about salary, benefits, the work environment, and other issues that may be relevant. When the interview is over, tell the candidate that you will be in touch with him or her, and explain that you are interviewing a number of other people for the position as well. The next steps:

- Evaluate the overall impression that each applicant has made on you.
- Narrow the list down to three or four candidates.
- Interview each of the finalists again, and try to conduct interviews that are more in-depth than your first ones were, probing to cover different subjects.

The final step—making a decision—is the toughest, but this is where you will either shine as an executive or fall by the wayside. But don't be paralyzed by the fear of making a mistake. Marcia Israel says, "I find that it's impossible to make the right hiring decision every time. When I am looking for a buyer, as an example, I could hire any of five different women who are just adequate, but I keep looking until I finally find the one who is creative. She is the one I stick with. I learned a long time ago that I must not keep people on our payroll who are just adequate. That's the easy way out, and if I settled for less than the high-caliber person I am always looking for, I would find myself burdened with a mediocre staff of buyers who would adversely affect our business."

Terrie Williams of Essence Communications told me, "One of my first tasks as a new manager was to find a public relations coordinator. I hired four different people on a temporary basis, and not one could handle what is actually a very demanding job. Finally, in desperation, I hired a white man, and for a while I wasn't sure in my own mind whether I wanted him to be successful in the job. How would he fit in as one of three whites in an organization of eighty blacks? What would my associates think about my hiring a white man? What would my management think? Well, he was and is up to the job. He is very comfortable working with a black woman as his boss, and my associates aren't interested in the color of his skin. He's getting the job done, and that's all any of us care about."

Suzanne de Passe says, "When I am at the point of hiring someone at Motown, I depend a great deal on my own perceptions and how I feel he will fit into the company. It's really not important whether I like the person or not. My final determination as to whether he will be hired or not is based on what I perceive to be the person's desire in life. What does he want? What is he looking for? I try to tap into his deeper self. I try to determine his level of personal integrity; that to me is all-important. I do a lot of listening, and then I come to a final decision."

FIRING

The heaviest price you must pay for being a manager is that you are forced to fire people. It is probably the most unpleasant, horrendous experience you will ever encounter during your entire career. Unless you are a completely callous, unfeeling person, you will go through agonies before you get to the point that you say to someone, "We have to let you go."

I have advised you to prepare yourself for various situations numerous times in this book, and dismissing someone is certainly one of the situations for which being prepared is essential. First, you must develop an exit interview scenario that permits the man or woman who is being let go to retain some degree of self-respect, one that prevents you from completely destroying the person's ego.

I've seen good ways and bad ways to fire people, but never any easy ways. I have wrestled with the problem of whether to tell the whole truth or not for many years, and I've finally concluded that, for me, it is better to tell a little white lie. To tell someone that he or she is incompetent is rather cruel and insensitive, so I skirt the issue by creating an impersonal, if fictional, situation. I say, "We are restructuring the department," or "Economic conditions demand that . . ." or, "We are taking the company in another direction," or something similar. I just can't bring myself to say to another human being, "You're lousy at your job, and that's why I'm firing you." Maybe the person thinks he knows the truth but hopes he's wrong. With my little white lie, I've at least given him the opportunity to save face in a situation that is very uncomfortable for both parties.

Marcia Israel agrees with me. She says, "I give it a lot of thought before I bring the unfortunate person in to give him the bad news. I figure out a good reason for my decision, which I would prefer to call subterfuge rather than dishonesty. I just omit certain facts. I omit telling the person that he has been doing his job badly. Instead I say that we are splitting the department in two, or that we are changing the structure, or that the profitability of the department is down and certain changes must be made. I always try to find a hurtless way of firing someone."

Terrie Williams told me, "The first time I had to fire someone was a nerve-wracking experience for me. I decided to take the gentle approach. I, in effect, took the blame myself and told her that it was my problem, that I had difficulty working with her. It took me two days to get her to make the decision to leave without my actually having to fire her. By trial and error I finally learned to be an effective boss, but there were many agonizing moments before I felt comfortable and attained a degree of confidence about the way I handled the job."

As the new director of the American Film Institute, one of Jean Firstenberg's first responsibilities was cutting staff. "When I first came on board and was told that I was a hundred fifty thousand dollars over budget, I automatically thought of ways to raise the money," she said. "I didn't want to think of the necessity for staff cutbacks, but I eventually learned that this was the wrong way to manage. I knew I had to steel myself to discharge people who were not absolutely essential to the operation. Although it was always difficult, my first experiences were not too bad because they were people I had not hired, and who had already been told they should not be on the AFI payroll.

But later on, when I was forced to let people go whom I had hired myself, guilt took over, and it was agonizing. To this day, it still is."

Motown executive Suzanne de Passe says, "I must be doing something right, because I've only fired four people in fourteen years. When I finally decide to discharge someone, I make sure that it doesn't come as a surprise. I alert the person that something is wrong, keep reminding, and when I finally give him the sad news, he is expecting it. I try to keep the conversation issue oriented, never personal. I try to release people with love. It's difficult to do, but I put a lot of effort into it."

It is always a good idea to give an employee clear indications of any performance problems and unambiguous warnings of impending dismissal. Not only will it make the exit interview less traumatic, but it establishes a solid case for your defense in the event that an ex-employee sues you for wrongful dismissal.

If one of your employees is not meeting the responsibilities of his job satisfactorily, take these steps:

- Deliver an oral warning. Tell the person that you are not pleased with his performance, and tell him why.
- Write a memo for your personal file that fully documents the dates and situations of the person's misconduct or mistakes.
- If performance does not improve after the first warning, meet again with the employee, and give him a specific deadline and objectives for improvement. Give him a written statement of the objectives and the deadline, and keep a copy in your file.
- If the second warning is not heeded, tell the employee that if his performance is not improved by a given date, he will be fired.

If, after all this, the person neither improves nor resigns, you have established sufficient grounds for dismissal to avoid or significantly reduce legal liability.

COMING TO TERMS WITH FAILURE

Every truly successful woman or man has experienced failures in the course of her or his career, and these failures actually help to give each a realistic perspective of the world in which she or he lives and works. If you are willing to take the risks that anyone who is building a career should and must take, then you must also expect occasional failures. Careers rarely if ever take off and remain forever on an unswerving upward course. Reverses and lateral moves will interrupt the essentially upward career path of a successful woman. The reverses should be expected, and the lateral moves can be considered holding periods until it is time for the next move forward.

Women who do take the necessary risks discover that these experiences provide important insights, which prove to be profitable additions to their total store of career knowledge.

You may find yourself totally discouraged when you learn that your number-one project, which you've been working on for many months, has been shot down by top management. Don't stew about it. Don't get depressed. If you ask your boss about this kind of setback, he'll probably admit that some of his pet ideas have gone down in flames too. You're not alone, so don't waste your energy bemoaning your fate. Move on to the next project.

If you are presently burdening yourself with fear of failure, you must shift gears and almost welcome your first serious setback, because then you will realize that it isn't that difficult to pick yourself up and go on. If you don't overcome your present fear, you will spend your entire career with a cloud of vague terror hanging over your head—certainly not a pleasant prospect. It's easy for me to tell you not to be afraid of failure, but unfortunately I can't tell you *how* to overcome your fear. It's a hard lesson, and one that every successful woman has had to master in her own way. The thing that is universal, however, is their agreement that everyone emerges from a business crisis a stronger and smarter business professional.

ROGERS' RULES FOR BEING THE BEST BOSS YOU CAN BE

1. Do unto your employees as you would have your boss do unto you.
2. Praise the work of employees who merit it—and praise them in public.
3. Sandwich any criticism between two layers of praise—and criticize in private.
4. Give your subordinates feedback and coaching.
5. Try to rule by consensus; encourage your subordinates to participate with you in decisions that involve them, making them understand, of course, that when there is a difference of opinion between you, the final decision must be yours.
6. Insist that you don't want to be surrounded by yes-men and yes-women. Encourage criticism and feedback from your staff to you.
7. Encourage your employees to ask questions and to alert you to potential problems before they erupt.
8. Establish an open-door policy. Isolation breeds stagnation.
9. Have a sense of humor about yourself.

10. Tell your subordinates the reasons for major decisions that create changes in the department.
11. Establish priorities for yourself, and make certain that you and your subordinates agree on what their priorities are.
12. Delegate authority and promote a certain degree of autonomy, but establish regular reporting procedures.
13. Trust people until they prove unworthy of your trust.
14. Be firm, be fair, be consistent.
15. Let your subordinates know that an occasional mistake isn't fatal. Every successful person knows that if you make decisions, you'll sometimes make mistakes.
16. Don't play favorites; treat everyone equally.
17. Treat your employees with respect.
18. Make each employee feel that he or she is an important member of your team.

Bibliography

Baer, Jean. *How To Be an Assertive (not aggressive) Woman.* New York City New American Library, 1976.

Bloom, Lynn Z., Karen Coburn, and Joan Perlman. *The New Assertive Woman.* New York: Dell, 1975.

Brown, Helen Gurley. *Having It All.* New York: Pocket Books, 1982.

Roman Gallese, Liz. *Women Like Us.* New York: William Morrow, 1985.

Harrigan, Bette Lehan. *Games Mother Taught You.* New York: Warner Books, 1977.

Hewlett, Sylvia Ann. *A Less Life.* New York: William Morrow, 1986.

Hodgkinson, Liz. *The Working Woman's Guide.* Wellingborough, England: Thorsons Publishers, 1985.

Josefowitz, Natasha *You're the Boss.* New York: Warner Books, 1985.

Loden, Marilyn. *Feminine Leadership.* New York: Times Books, 1985.

MacDonald, Janet W. *Climbing the Ladder.* London: Methuen 1986.

Miles, Rosalind. *Danger—Men At Work.* London: MacDonald & Co., 1983.

Nierenberg, Juliet, and Irene S. Ross. *Women and the Art of Negotiating.* New York: Simon & Schuster, 1985.

Phelps, Stanlee, and Nancy Austin. *The Assertive Woman.* San Luis Obispo: Impact Publishers, 1975.

Steckert, Kathryn. *Sweet Success.* New York: Macmillan, 1986.

Index

235